MINDELL'S
PROCESS-ORIENTED PSYCHOLOGY

THEORETICAL FOUNDATIONS

Other Books by Alan James Strachan and Janet Coster:

*The Lure of the Ring:
Power, Addiction and Transcendence
in Tolkien's The Lord of the Rings*

MINDELL'S
PROCESS-ORIENTED PSYCHOLOGY

THEORETICAL FOUNDATIONS

by

ALAN JAMES STRACHAN, PH.D.

Leaping Panther Press

Copyright © 2022 by Alan James Strachan and Janet Coster
All rights reserved.

ISBN-13 (trade paperback): 978-1-7323156-2-4
ISBN-13 (eBook): 978-1-7323156-3-1

In accordance with the U.S. Copyright Act of 1976, the scanning, uploading, and electronic sharing of any part of this book without permission of the publisher constitute unlawful piracy and theft of the author's intellectual property. No part of this book may be reproduced or transmitted in any form or by any means, electronic or mechanical, including photocopying, recording, or by any information storage and retrieval system, except for excerpts used for reviews, without permission in writing from the publisher.

Published by Leaping Panther Press

Cover artwork by Cynthia Blair

Book design by Bri Bruce Productions

"An outstanding exploration of the philosophy and practice of Mindell's Process Work paradigm. Dr. Strachan lucidly and succinctly explains the principles and nuances of the Analytical Psychology of Carl Jung, Gestalt Psychology, Modern Physics, Taoism, Neuro-Linguistic Programming and Information Theory and describes how each of these elements are mirrored in Mindell's universal approach. Indispensable for practitioners of POP and for all others interested in psychology, psychotherapy or personal growth."

— Max Schupbach, Ph.D., Deep Democracy Institute, Process Work Diplomate

"If you are curious about Arnold Mindell's Process Work and/or the creative leading edge of the work of Carl Jung, this small book is essential. More than a comparison, it is an invitation with gravitational force, a worm hole that draws you into some of the most important and rarely-explored dimensions of human psychology, the nature of information, and the intersections of physics and the mind/body questions. Enjoy."

— John Mizelle, M.F.T., Process Work Diplomate

"Dr. Strachan has done a masterful job, offering a unique, detail-oriented, organized and important contribution to the field. A remarkably cogent, eloquent, insightful book. Essential reading for practitioners of Process Work, as well as an inviting doorway for anyone interested in an approach to psychotherapy that honors the client's inner wisdom and innate capacity for self-transformation."

— Nisha Zenoff, Ph.D., Process Work Diplomate

ACKNOWLEDGEMENTS

I am deeply grateful to my wife, Janet Coster, for impeccable editing, invaluable advice on the cover design, and—not incidentally—for keeping me as close to sane as humanly possible.

Once again I am greatly indebted to Cynthia Blair for her exceptional artwork in creating the cover illustration.

TABLE OF CONTENTS

INTRODUCTION 1

CHAPTER 1

The Roots of Process Work in the Analytical Psychology of
C. G. Jung................................. 5
    Introduction 5
    Teleology 5
        The Teleological Perspective of Jung 7
        The Teleological Perspective of Mindell 7
    Therapist-Client Relationship 9
        Jung's Views of the Therapist-Client Relationship 9
        Mindell's Views of the Therapist-Client Relationship 13
    The Body in Therapy 20
        Jung and the Body 20
        Mindell and the Body 24
    Historical Foundations: Taoism 26
        Introduction 26
        Taoism: Jung 27
        Taoism: Mindell 30
    Historical Foundations: Alchemy 32
        The Historical Background of Alchemy 32
        Jung's Approach to Alchemy 33
        Mindell's Use of the Alchemical Paradigm 34

CHAPTER 2

Exploring the Connections Between Psychology and Physics 37
    Introduction 37
    Classical Physics 39
    Modern Physics 40
        Process as a Unifying Concept 46
        Bringing Relativity into Psychology 48
        The Phenomenological Attitude 50
        Modern Physics and the Body 51
        The Individual's Relationship to the World 53
            Field Theory 54
            The Hologram 55

CHAPTER 3

The Importance of Information Theory to Process Work ... 59
    Introduction 59
    The Development of Information Theory 59
    Key Concepts 60
    Information Theory and Process Work 60
        Recognition of the Fundamental Importance of Process 62
        Emphasis Upon Principles of Organization 63
        The Systems Perspective 63
        The Significance of Feedback 66
        The Information Value of Events 67
    Conclusion 68

CHAPTER 4

Gestalt Psychology: Extraverting the Unconscious 69
    Introduction 69
    Techniques of Gestalt Therapy 69
    Gestalt Therapy and Process-Oriented Psychology . . . 70

CHAPTER 5

Neuro-Linguistic Programming: Behavior as a Window to the Unconscious 73
    Introduction 73
    Channel Structure 73
    Emphasis Upon Sensory-Based Information 75
    Methods of Establishing Rapport 76
    Awareness of the Channels 77
    The Importance of the Lesser-Used Channels 77
    Conscious and Unconscious 78
    Conclusion 79

REFERENCES 81

APPENDIX A

Jung and Mindell: Common Terminology 87

APPENDIX B

Terminology of Process-Oriented Psychology 89

About the Author 97

MINDELL'S
PROCESS-ORIENTED PSYCHOLOGY

THEORETICAL FOUNDATIONS

by

ALAN JAMES STRACHAN, PH.D.

INTRODUCTION

When I was first licensed as a psychotherapist I knew a fair amount about the theory and practice of psychotherapy, but I was uncertain how everything I had learned fit together, and how, as a practical matter, I should apply the different theories and practices.

I had been very interested in somatic processes, so I trained in a number of hands-on bodywork modalities. I also had been trained in both individual and group facilitation. I practiced a relational style of psychotherapy, listening carefully, communicating empathy, tracking and taking into account both the client's and my own responses. I had been trained in transpersonal psychology, so I was aware of the developmental continuum that extends from the neurotic and psychotic patterns of thought and behavior emphasized by Western psychology, to capacities for highly developed self-awareness, integration and self-transcendence emphasized by Eastern psychology. I had learned a number of systems of psychological typology, such as the Enneagram, Myers-Briggs, and the DSM (Diagnostic and Statistical Manual of Mental Disorders). I also had some awareness of how cultural, political and economic events, practices and beliefs shape individual psyches.

All of this was well and good. What was confusing to me, however, was that I had very little understanding about how to integrate what I knew. I needed a road map, a coherent and integrated system of psychotherapy that took into account somatic, relational, group, world, and psychospiritual factors. Above all, I wanted that road map to reflect a deep respect for the client.

Fortunately, shortly after licensure I began to study

Process-Oriented Psychology with Arnold Mindell. I found Process Work (as it also came to be known) to be one of the most innovative and integrative methods of psychotherapy I had encountered. It was comprehensive, adaptable, singularly focusing on the client's experience arising moment to moment, and completely trusting that the client's process contained an innate wisdom that could guide the psychotherapy and facilitate healing.

After some years of study, I wrote a doctoral dissertation on Process Work entitled *The Dreaming Body: A Case Study of the Relationship Between Chronic Body Symptoms and Childhood Dreams According to Process-Oriented Psychology*.

In the dissertation I investigated the relationship between childhood dreams and the subsequent appearance of chronic body symptoms in adulthood. Process Work theory, following Jung, held that childhood dreams reveal fundamental life patterns or life myths. The life myth may then manifest in adulthood in a variety of chronic patterns, including as chronic body symptoms. Process-Oriented Psychology also maintains that there is a process structure to all experience, and that a childhood dream and an adult chronic body symptom are related through this structure.

My research led me to analyze a videotape of a psychotherapy session conducted in accord with the principles and methods of Process-Oriented Psychology in which the client worked on both an adult chronic body symptom and a childhood dream. The findings suggested that the childhood dream and chronic body symptom conveyed the same information; that they each were reflections of a more fundamental process; and that the dream appeared to anticipate the subsequent development of the body symptom.

Above and beyond requirements for the dissertation, I also researched and wrote an extensive appendix in which I described the theoretical foundations of process work, focusing on the work of Carl Jung, modern physics, information theory, gestalt psychology, and neuro-linguistic programming (NLP).

Several teachers at the Process Work Institute used my appendix to teach students. Now, many years later, I have decided to publish the theoretical foundation chapters as a stand-alone book so that it will be readily available to students of Process-Oriented Psychology as well as to anyone interested in the theoretical foundations of the work.

Alan James Strachan

2022

CHAPTER 1
THE ANALYTICAL PSYCHOLOGY OF C. G. JUNG

Introduction

After receiving a Master's Degree in physics, Mindell went to the Jung Institute in Zurich to study Analytical Psychology. He became a Diplomate and a training analyst, and, as a result, the influence of Jung's work runs very deeply through Process-Oriented Psychology. Mindell writes, "I call process-oriented psychology a daughter of Jung's because even though she is now growing up and carrying her own name, she comes from his household. His blood, spirit and history are hers as well." (1988b, p. 2)

In this section, I highlight the principle concepts of Jung's work that have a direct bearing on Process-Oriented Psychology: the teleological perspective, the therapist-client relationship, the body in therapy, historical foundations (Taoism and alchemy), and common terminology.

Teleology

The history of epistemology has been characterized by the contrasting attempts of determinism and teleology to explain natural phenomena. Determinism is the philosophical doctrine that every event, act, and decision is the inevitable consequence of antecedents that are independent of the human will, while teleology is the use of ultimate purpose or design as a means of explaining natural phenomena.

The deterministic orientation explains an event by looking for prior events that lead up to and cause it. The assumption is that there is an unbroken chain of events, one leading to another, which explain the event in question.

In the field of psychology, Freud's orientation was largely deterministic. His approach had been to psychoanalyze a symptom by uncovering the relevant personal events that preceded and presumably caused it. In practical terms, this often meant tracing symptoms back to their origins in childhood.

The value of this orientation is that it encourages the therapist to uncover any prior events that are relevant to the problem at hand. The potential drawback of a strictly deterministic approach is, however, that problems tend to be reduced to constituent elements and are fit into convenient categories. A given experience will tend to be seen as pathological - as a problem caused by specific events - and its potential value ignored. The meaning of a symptom is derived from the events that gave rise to it.

The teleological orientation approaches a symptom by attempting to discover its underlying purpose or meaning. Teleology assumes that a symptom is an indication of a process that is still unfolding. The advantage of this approach is that it automatically places a constructive, growth-oriented value on any problem or symptom. The potential drawback, of course, is that a strictly teleological orientation may overlook important antecedent events that have a bearing on the situation.

The Teleological Perspective of Jung

Jung believed that there was evidence of teleology in the purposive behavior of neurotic symptoms and complexes, in synchronistic events, and in the individuation process generally (Jung, 1933, 1953b, 1969). For example, he wrote that ". . . It is correct that neurotic symptoms and complexes are also elaborate 'arrangements' which inexorably pursue their aims, with incredible obstinacy and cunning. Neurosis is teleologically oriented" (Jung, 1953b, p. 39).

Jung's teleological orientation meant that he viewed problems and symptoms as meaningful and purposeful, i.e. that they were indications of the psyche's movement toward integration and wholeness. Even in his work with 'incurable' institutionalized patients, Jung assumed that there was a germ of meaning in their hallucinations and paranoid ideas. By investigating and trying to understand the world of his patients, Jung discovered that a life history and a pattern of hopes and desires lay behind the psychosis. Discovering the meaning of the symptoms made communication possible and improvement more likely.

Jung did not try to replace causal explanations with teleological ones. Rather he thought that both were necessary in order to have a complete understanding of a situation. Thus, he wrote that "In psychology one ought to be as wary of believing absolutely in causality as of an absolute belief in teleology" (1953b, p. 289).

The Teleological Perspective of Mindell

Mindell has been greatly influenced by Jung's teleological

perspective. In Coma, he wrote that "My background in process work is based upon the finalistic philosophy applied by Jung to psychological situations" (1989a, p. 27).

Mindell considers all symptoms as positive in the sense that they carry information which, if processed and integrated, furthers individuation. His writings repeatedly underscore the importance of the teleological orientation to Process-Oriented Psychology. *Dreambody* and *Working With the Dreaming Body* are concerned with finding the meaning behind physical symptoms. *Coma* describes methods for discovering the purpose and aiding the unfolding of comatose states. The thesis of *River's Way* is that the accurate observation of the client combined with the ability to support that which is being observed will promote a useful development of the client's process. *City Shadows* is an exploration of the process structure and underlying meaning of conditions such as psychosis, catatonia, depression, and mania.

Mindell's commitment to the teleological perspective is one of the main ways in which Process-Oriented Psychology is different from most other schools of psychology. Even the most subtle or unusual signals, from the flutter of a comatose patient's eyelid to synchronistic events, can be regarded as meaningful. This means that the Process-Oriented Therapist must be prepared to notice, support, and try to understand any experience of the client. The teleological approach challenges the therapist to maintain an attitude of open-mindedness and caring, to have faith that something useful will develop by taking such an approach, and to be willing to develop along with the client.

The Therapist-Client Relationship

Jung's Views of the Therapist-Client Relationship

In his essay entitled "Problems of Modern Psychotherapy" (1966a), Jung wrote that the process of psychotherapy has four main components: confession, elucidation, education, and transformation.

The goal of **confession** is to bring to awareness material that the client has repressed. Jung used the term 'shadow' to refer to the personal material that is unacceptable to the client's conscious identity, or persona. Recognizing and admitting shadow material to the therapist often has a cathartic or cleansing effect. The principle underlying such confession is that awareness is healing, i.e., that secrets that remain unconscious are more likely to cause problems than those that are consciously acknowledged.

Moving deeper, the stage of **elucidation** involves a resolution of the transference, or the client's projection (or transfer) of unresolved unconscious material onto the therapist. Jung believed that the transference was not only the projection of the client's original, unresolved issues with the parents (as maintained by Freud), but in addition, that the client's projections could contain seeds of unrealized psychological growth which were constellated around the archetypes of the collective unconscious. Thus in Jung's view the transference material could either be personal or archetypal, and the therapist had to be prepared to deal with either eventuality.

In the **education** stage, the therapist and client address the issue of how the client is to integrate his or her newfound awareness into the social fabric of his or her life.

At this point, the client must learn how to apply the inner work in such a way as to be adapted to society.

It is in the final stage, **transformation**, that Jung truly addressed the nature of the therapist-client relationship. This is the stage in which the client must consider if it is enough to be a 'normal' and adapted social being. Jung wrote that, for many, social adaptation is easy, but that it may not address all of the individual's needs. Those who cannot adapt without sacrificing essential and important parts of themselves must learn to become "appropriately non-adapted" (1966a, p. 72).

The therapist faces two challenges in this stage of transformation. The first challenge is to support the client's unique path of growth, and the second is to be willing to change along with the client.

First, Jung believed that the therapist had to learn to recognize and support the individual needs of clients. This meant the therapist had to make every attempt to follow the individual client's process, repeatedly discarding hypotheses in order to be faithful to what was actually occurring:

> It is enough to drive one to despair that in practical psychology there are no universally valid recipes and rules. There are only individual cases with the most heterogeneous needs and demands—so heterogeneous that we can virtually never know in advance what course a given case will take, for which reason it is better for the doctor to abandon all preconceived notions. This does not mean that he should throw them overboard, but that in any given case he should use them merely as hypotheses for a possible explanation. (Jung, 1966a, p. 71)

By not following a predetermined formula, Jung placed his faith in the client's individuation process to ultimately determine the direction of the therapy. Thus, he wrote that "In dealing with psychological developments, the doctor should, as a matter of principle, let nature rule and himself do his utmost to avoid influencing the patient in the direction of his own philosophical, social, and political bent" (1966a, p. 26).

Here arises the second challenge for the therapist, for it is a common occurrence that, in the course of therapy, the therapist's own unresolved issues, i.e., the counter-transference, could emerge. In addition to the professional relationship between therapist and client, Jung believed that the mutual influence that gives rise to the transference and counter-transference also made the encounter a very personal one.

> For, twist and turn the matter as we may, the relation between doctor and patient remains a personal one within the impersonal framework of professional treatment. By no device can the treatment be anything but the product of mutual influence, in which the whole being of the doctor as well as that of the patient plays its part. (Jung, 1966a, p. 71)

According to Whitmont (1969), Jung was the first to break with traditional psychoanalysis by eliminating the therapist's couch, preferring instead to sit face-to-face with his clients. This practice heightened the personal nature of the interaction.

In order to cope with the counter-transference and therefore better serve the client, Jung believed that the therapist continually had to be willing to work on the therapist's own issues. To this end, Jung was the first to require that aspiring therapists receive personal psychotherapy as part of their training: "The analyst is blind to the attitude of his patient to the exact extent that he does not see himself and his own unconscious problems. For this reason, I maintain that a doctor must himself be analyzed before he practices analysis" (Jung, 1970a, p. 235). In addition, while conducting a psychotherapy session the therapist had to be willing to constantly examine himself or herself, and to do so while remaining aware of the client's process.

> The analyst must go on learning endlessly, and never forget that each new case brings new problems to light and thus gives rise to unconscious assumptions that have never before been constellated. We could say, without too much exaggeration, that a good half of every treatment that probes at all deeply consists in the doctor's examining himself, for only what he can put right in himself can he hope to put right in the patient. (1966a, p. 116)

It is not enough to maintain an impervious facade and apply techniques from a safe psychological distance. Instead the personality of the therapist - the range and depth of the therapist's humanity - is a significant factor in the treatment of the client. This tenet effectively removes psychotherapy from the medical model, for it no longer is simply a case of the healthy doctor treating the sick patient. More fundamentally, it is an encounter between two human beings, both of whom become transformed.

Mindell's Views of the Therapist-Client Relationship

Mindell tends to describe therapist-client interactions in terms of process structure rather than as transference and counter-transference phenomena. He has included in the channel structure of Process-Oriented Psychology a composite channel termed "relationship." Relationship can refer to any one-to-one relationship, including interactions between therapist and client. In this chapter, I consider first the client's reactions to the therapist and then the therapist's reactions to the client.

The client's reactions to the therapist fall into three general categories: complete projection, wholly accurate observation, or a combination of the two.

If the client is projecting, then in accord with Jung, Process-Oriented Psychology maintains that the material either can be personal or archetypal. When the client is projecting, the therapist can point out the act of projection and its nature can be explored. This constitutes a standard exchange between therapist and client in Process-Oriented Psychology as well as in many other schools of psychotherapy.

But what of a situation in which the client's reaction represents a partially or completely accurate description of the therapist? In such a case, the therapist must decide whether or not to admit that the client has made an accurate observation. In making this decision, the therapist will be influenced by his or her psychotherapeutic model.

In some schools of psychotherapy, the therapist always would reflect the client's remarks back to the client, and never would admit that there was some truth in what the client said. This approach maintains a hierarchical split between therapist and client in which the client is regarded always as projecting and the therapist is seen as a perfect mirror, one who never has anything personal to reveal. This type of exchange does not acknowledge the relational aspect of client-therapist interactions.

In Process-Oriented Psychology, by contrast, the therapist examines himself or herself to discover whether the client's remarks are accurate. If so, then in some cases it is appropriate to distinguish with the client what is projection and what is not. Mindell described a hypothetical case of a woman who notices she is mentally criticizing herself. Encouraged to listen to her internal critic,

> Then she might say, "Oh, my stomach hurts." Now she's switched to the proprioceptive channel. "What does that feel like?" I might ask. "Well, it feels bad," she says, making a fist at the same time. So we focus on the fist, which is a kinesthetic or movement expression of the same process. Then I might have her amplify the fist by making a muscle in her bicep, tightening her neck, and tensing her face. Suddenly she says, "Now I look like my father." "What does he look like?" I ask. "He looks like you!" At this point, I would probably say, "Can't we take this inward? Does it really have to be projected outward. Are you really criticizing me?' . . . Then as a therapist I have to look inside myself and see whether a part of me isn't in fact critical of her. There may be, in which case, I need to recognize and talk about that part. We may go back and forth until the person realizes that I'm not like her father, but the fatherlike part is in her. (Bodian, 1990, p. 69)

This is an example of therapist and client working in the relationship channel. The therapist's willingness to engage in this way provides a reality check for the client, who would otherwise have to doubt either her own beliefs or the therapist's honesty. Such a disclosure by the therapist promotes trust and can deepen the rapport between them.

In this example, the therapist tracked the signals from internal auditory (hearing the critic) to proprioception (stomach) to kinesthetic (fist) to visual (seeing her father) to relationship. By closely following signals and analyzing the underlying process structure, the process worker has a rationale for making interventions with the client. In this case, the need for relationship work emerged in an organic fashion as the therapist followed the client's process.

In Process-Oriented Psychology, as this example indicates, the therapist must consider all sources of information as potentially relevant, *including the therapist's own reactions to the client*. Mindell differentiates two categories of reactions that the therapist may have toward the client: counter-transference and being "dreamed up."

Counter-transference, as defined in the preceding section, refers to those instances in which the therapist's unresolved personal material is projected onto the client. The Process-Oriented therapist is expected to notice and work internally with his or her own counter-transference reactions while at the same time tracking the client's process. As in the example described above, the signals and process structure will indicate whether it is appropriate to disclose counter-transference material.

The second category of the therapist's reactions consists of what Mindell calls "dreamed up reactions." For example, imagine a psychotherapy session in which a male client is describing how he was betrayed by a business associate. He says that although the associate was a close friend, and betrayal was devastating, he has thought it through and decided that business is business and it is best to put the event behind him. As he recounts the incident and his "concluding" thought, he is very rational and his voice is measured. At the same time his face is slightly flushed and he appears to be somewhat short of breath. The therapist listening to the account begins to get angry, and it is all the therapist can do to keep from denouncing the business associate and suggesting ways of remedying the situation. The therapist is being "dreamed up" to have this reaction.

Analyzing the process structure reveals that the client is sending a double signal. Double signaling, one of the key concepts in Process-Oriented Psychology, refers to instances in which the client simultaneously is sending two contradictory signals. Typically, the client will be aware of one of the messages (i.e., the one with which they consciously identify) and unaware of the other. The "double" signal specifically refers to the message that the client is unaware that he or she also is sending.

In this example, on the surface (the primary process), the client is calm, rational, and accepting, but underneath (the secondary process), he is furious. The therapist unconsciously notices the facial flush and shortness of breath and reacts to these signals by feeling the anger that the client is expressing only indirectly. At the moment, the client is unaware of his anger; it is like a dream he is having unconsciously. The therapist unknowingly begins to react like the client's secondary - or dream-like part - that is, the therapist is "dreamed up." The therapist has become a channel for the client's secondary process. (It is important to distinguish that Process-Oriented Psychology assigns nearly the opposite meanings to the terms primary and secondary process as did Freud. This is discussed in more detail in the Appendix B.)

It is very helpful if the therapist is able to differentiate between counter-transference and being dreamed up. Mindell wrote that

> As long as the therapist has a reaction which is short-lived and lasts only as long as he is in the vicinity of the client, we can speak of a purely dreamed-up reaction. If, however, this reaction lasts longer than the time of the interview, we must also consider the possibility that the therapist is unconsciously projecting something of himself onto his client . . . We speak of dreaming up when the therapist has no affects before, after, or as soon as the dreamer has integrated and understood his dream material. (1985a, p. 43)

If the therapist suspects that he or she is getting dreamt up, the therapist fairly safely can assume that he or she has missed a double signal. The task then is to discover the signal and encourage the client to express the unconscious material more congruently. As the client takes over his or her secondary process, the therapist's urge to express this aspect of the dreaming process will diminish. (Note: the psychoanalytic concept of projective identification is similar to that of dreaming up, but a crucial distinction is discussed in the chapter on Information Theory.)

Complicating the interaction enormously is the fact that dreaming up and projection can happen simultaneously in both therapist and client. The therapist's ability to unravel such complex interactions will be greatly enhanced if the therapist can differentiate counter-transference from dreaming up, and is able to attend closely to the complex, subtle, and ongoing flow of signals.

The therapist's level of awareness and flexibility in relating to the client will be determined by the therapist's edges, that is, by the limits of the therapist's own identity. Goodbread (1987, 1989) has categorized the kinds of edges the therapist may encounter. Two of these - personal and professional edges - have been alluded to previously. The personal edges include the therapist's unresolved characterological issues and his or her least accessible channel (for an explanation of channels, please refer to the Appendix B). Professional edges will vary according to the therapist's psychotherapeutic model and will affect attitudes toward therapist-client interactions, including counter-transference phenomena. In addition, every therapist is influenced by cultural edges in which habitual and typically unconscious acceptance of cultural norms limits awareness.

In summary, it is apparent that Mindell has been influenced considerably by Jung's views of the therapist-client relationship. This may be an important reason why Mindell developed a relationship channel as an integral part of the theoretical and practical structure of Process-Oriented Psychology. Some areas of overlap include an emphasis upon (1) identifying and supporting the needs of the client; (2) discarding hypotheses if they do not accurately describe the client; (3) recognition that transference projections may either be personal or archetypal in nature; (4) the need for the therapist to work on himself or herself both between and during sessions; and, when appropriate, (5) going beyond the role of therapist to convey personal information or feelings. Implicit in Mindell's approach, as with Jung's, is a trust in the client's individuation process to provide guidance for both therapist and client. Jung and Mindell both refer to psychotherapy as a process of observing and following nature.

Although Mindell's basic philosophy of and approach to the therapist-client relationship is similar to Jung's, there are some important differences. One of these differences is the degree to which Mindell has integrated an information theory perspective by focusing on signals, information flow, and feedback. This gives Process-Oriented Psychology a behaviorist flavor, although some behaviorally-oriented models of psychotherapy, such as Neuro-Linguistic Programming, do not regard relationship work between therapist and client as necessary or appropriate. Mindell has, instead, used awareness of the signal flow as a rationale for and a means of focusing upon the nuances of relationship work between therapist and client.

Mindell's other major contribution to therapist-client interactions is his theory of dreaming up. This concept allows the Process-Oriented therapist to differentiate the therapist's own counter-transference projections from any reactions triggered by the client's double signals. This in turn enables the therapist to focus on and help the client access the material being expressed through their own secondary signal. A signal-based awareness of therapist-client interactions combined with a willingness to engage the client in a personal manner help the Process-Oriented therapist to know when it is appropriate to discuss counter-transference reactions with the client, and to know when personal reactions are in fact a "dreamed up" aspect of the client's process.

The Body in Therapy

Jung and the Body

References to the body appear throughout Jung's writings. For example, he conducted word association experiments in which he established a connection between psychological complexes and physiological changes. In one of these studies, he used a galvanometer to measure electrical skin resistance. ("On Psychophysical Relations of the Associative Experiment," Jung, 1973) In another study, he used a galvanometer and a pneumograph designed to measure the frequency and amplitude of breathing. ("Further Investigations of the Galvanic Phenomenon and Respiration in Normal and Insane Individuals," Jung & Ricksher, 1973).

Due to their autonomous nature, complexes manifest as both psychological and somatic symptoms. The physiological effect of complexes is not limited to changes in breathing and electrical skin resistance; in addition, they can "disturb the conscious performance . . . produce disturbances of memory and blockages in the flow of associations . . . temporarily obsess consciousness, or influence speech and action in an unconscious way." (Jung, 1969, p. 121).

Jung also hypothesized the presence of a toxic factor in the pathogenesis of schizophrenia. In an article on "The Psychology of Dementia Praecox" (Jung, 1960), he suggested that such a toxin could play a role in the fixation of the complex, thereby contributing to the perseveration of symptoms.

Often studying the body language of his patients, Jung's first psychological study included observations of unconscious body movements (Jung, 1970b). While working at the Burgholzli Psychiatric Clinic in Zurich, he studied the perseverating gestures of regressed patients. One of his techniques was to closely watch silent, withdrawn patients, even those who had not spoken for years. When they moved or changed expression, he would imitate them, note his inner experience, and put this experience into words. In a number of cases, the patient would respond, a dialogue would be established, and the patient would improve (Van Der Post, 1977).

Jung recognized that for some patients movement was the ideal mode of self-expression. His writings contain a number of references to body movement as a form of active imagination (Jung, 1969, 1976). When appropriate Jung encouraged his patients to dance the mandala symbolisms which emerged in therapy:

> Among my patients I have come across cases of women who did not draw mandalas but danced them instead. In India there is a special name for this: mandala nrithya, the mandala dance. The dance figures express the same meanings as the drawings. My patients can say very little about the meaning of the symbols but are fascinated by them and find that they somehow express and have an effect on their subjective state. (Jung, 1967, p. 23)

A similar reference is also contained in *Dream Analysis* (Jung, 1984), while Van Der Post described Jung's dance movement interactions with a patient in a different context (1977).

Frequently theorizing about the nature of the mind-body relationship (Adler, 1975; Jung, 1966a; 1969,; 1967; 1959b), Jung's perspective is summarized in the following quotation from *Modern Man In Search of a Soul*:

> The distinction between mind and body is an artificial dichotomy, a discrimination which is unquestionably based far more on the peculiarity of intellectual understanding than on the nature of things. In fact, so intimate is the intermingling of bodily and psychic traits that not only can we draw far-reaching inferences as to the constitution of the psyche from the constitution of the body, but we can also infer from psychic peculiarities the corresponding bodily characteristics. (1973, p. 74)

In addition to Jung's consideration of complexes, he formulated a number of other concepts that addressed the unity of mind and body.

Jung theorized that archetypes bridged the mind-body dichotomy at the psychoid level. The psychoid is the deepest level of the unconscious and is completely inaccessible to consciousness. It has properties in common with the organic world, and is therefore both psychological and physiological in nature. Jung imagined a spectrum of consciousness ranging from an infra-red or physiological pole to an ultra-violet or spiritual/imagistic pole (Jung, 1969). On a theoretical level, the archetypes span both poles, and can thus be understood to bridge the mind/body dichotomy. On a practical level, the archetypes can manifest in behavior and physical symptoms.

Jung's idea of synchronicity also addressed the mind/body connection. In the broadest sense, synchronicity refers to a connection between subjective, psychological realities and events in the external, material world.

> ... it is not only possible but fairly probable, even, that psyche and matter are two different aspects of one and the same thing. The synchronicity phenomena point, it seems to me, in this direction, for they show that the nonpsychic can behave like the psychic, and vice versa, without there being any causal connection between them. (1969, p. 215)

A number of Jung's followers have applied the concept of synchronicity to the relationship between psychological events and organic illness (Lockhart, 1977; Meier, 1986; Ziegler, 1962).

In the Tavistock Lectures, delivered in 1935, Jung described how the psychological concept of the shadow can manifest as body symptoms:

> We do not like to look at the shadow-side of ourselves; therefore, there are many people in our civilized society who have lost their shadow altogether, they have got rid of it. They are only two-dimensional; they have lost the third dimension, and with it they have usually lost the body. The body is a most doubtful friend because it produces things we do not like; there are too many things about the body which cannot be mentioned. The body is very often the personification of this shadow of the ego. (Jung, 1976, p. 23)

Finally, Jung pointed out that the ancient traditions of alchemy, Taoism, and the *Tibetan Book of the Dead* refer to a *corpus subtile*, a "subtle body" or "breath body" (Jung, 1953a, p. 408). The subtle body is a transfigured and resurrected body, that is, a body that is comprised of both matter and spirit.

To summarize, Jung was aware of and flexible enough to incorporate body-oriented approaches into the practice of psychotherapy. He discovered complexes by means of galvanic skin response, attended to movements and facial expressions, and encouraged clients to dance when that mode of self-expression seemed most appropriate. On a theoretical level, Jung's consideration of mind/body phenomena included concepts such as complexes, archetypes, the psychoid unconscious, the shadow, and synchronicity.

Jung did not, however, make body-oriented approaches a formal, explicit aspect of analytical psychology. If he systematized his approach, he did not write it down for others to follow. Nevertheless, his approach to psychotherapy and the scope of his theorizing created a climate sympathetic to the integration of body-oriented approaches with traditional forms of psychotherapy. One indication of this is the subsequent development of Jungian dance-movement therapy; another is Mindell's Process-Oriented Psychology.

Mindell and the Body

Mindell's studies at the Jung Institute in Zurich trained him to work with dreams and to be able to work on himself through active imagination. Excited about working with dream material, Mindell began to wonder

> whether what I now knew about dreams could be used also in working with the body and with relationships. I became frustrated with just sitting and talking; I was

fascinated with gestures, symptoms, odd or insistent physical sensations, and the different ways clients (for instance couples) had of relating to me and to each other. (Mindell, 1988b, p. 2)

Mindell's motivation to discover how to work with body symptoms increased when he became ill. His readings in psychology and Western medicine left him thinking that there were many methods of manipulating the body, but that he still did not know how to discover what his body was trying to say. He began to take careful notes on the body language of his clients, and soon noticed the tendency of many people to amplify their symptoms, actually making them more acute. He worked with terminally ill patients, encouraging them to amplify their physical symptoms, and discovered that illness is a meaningful condition and that amplification is a way to discover that meaning.

While working with a dying patient, Mindell realized that the man had had a dream that conveyed the same information elicited by amplifying his physical symptoms. Extrapolating from this, Mindell realized that dreams mirror body symptoms, and body symptoms mirror dreams, a discovery that he has subsequently corroborated with many other patients. From this insight, Mindell had the idea that there must be a 'dreambody' - an entity that simultaneously was both dream and body. Inspired by Jung, the dreambody is a reformulation of the concept of the subtle body mentioned in the preceding section.

Mindell's study of body language has ranged from overt signals such as posture, movement, and facial expressions to minimal cues such as pupil dilation and changes in skin color. Awareness of such body language is a critical component in the Process-Oriented therapist's ability to detect many double signals, in which, for example, the verbal content conflicts with nonverbal behavior.

Analyzing the process structure of a psychotherapy session, it is very common to discover that the secondary process (i.e., the process that is further from consciousness and therefore contains the seeds of growth) is located in proprioception or kinesthesia. This fact increases the importance of being able to recognize and work with somatic processes.

In short, the awareness and incorporation of somatic phenomena is an integral aspect of the theory and practice of Process-Oriented Psychology. While Jung included body-oriented approaches in his methods of working with patients, and clearly created a climate that encouraged further exploration, Mindell has explored somatic phenomena in far greater depth. Mindell's application of the channel system, his use of amplification, and his development of the concept of the dreambody has created a psychotherapeutic system that is both precise and adaptable when dealing with the spectrum of body/mind experience.

Historical Foundations: Taoism

Introduction

In his acknowledgments for the book, River's Way, Mindell wrote that he was indebted to Jung for introducing him to alchemy and Taoism, and that these two bodies of knowledge represent the historical foundations of Process-Oriented Psychology. According to Mindell, "Alchemy is based upon cooking what is incomplete and Taoism encourages one to discover the patterns behind reality and to follow their unfolding with appreciation and awareness" (1988a, p. 27). In this section, I briefly describe Jung's interest in alchemy and Taoism, and outline their respective importance to Process-Oriented Psychology.

Taoism: Jung

Jung was well into his career before he discovered parallels between the Chinese philosophy of Taoism and the theory and practice of analytical psychology. His writings on Taoism are primarily focused on Lao Tsu and on two Chinese texts: the *The Secret of the Golden Flower*, and the *I Ching*, or *Book of Changes*.

Jung believed that *The Secret of the Golden Flower* contained a description of the same process of individuation that he had observed in his clients. Jung saw this as evidence to support his theory of the collective unconscious, which he defined as the common substratum of the psyche that transcends all differences in culture and consciousness. According to Jung's theory, if consciousness becomes estranged from the archetypes of the collective unconscious, then a breakdown of the personality is likely to occur. What is then needed is a re-unification of the personal and collective elements of the psyche. Jung believed that such a unification of opposites was the issue that is addressed by Taoism generally and by *The Secret of the Golden Flower* in particular.

In his commentary on *The Secret of the Golden Flower*, Jung describes the essence of the Tao from a psychological perspective:

> If we take the Tao to be the method or conscious way by which to unite what is separated, we have probably come close to the psychological content of the concept .... There can be no doubt, either, that the realization of the opposite hidden in the unconscious—the process of "reversal"—signifies reunion with the unconscious laws of our being, and the purpose of this reunion is the attainment of conscious life or, expressed in Chinese terms, the realization of the Tao. (Jung, 1967, p. 21)

Thus, for Jung, the Tao is the process whereby opposites are reconciled within the psyche. In Jung's Analytical Psychology, this reconciliation is brought about by the transcendent function. Over time, the transcendent function, which is the tendency of the psyche to move toward wholeness and balance, fosters the individuation process.

It is important to note that the unfolding of the Tao and the process of individuation take into account not only intrapsychic processes but also meaningful events in the world. In Volume 7 of his *Collected Works*, Jung wrote:

> From a consideration of the claims of the inner and outer worlds, or rather, from the conflicts between them, the possible and the necessary follows. Unfortunately, our Western mind, lacking all culture in this respect, has never yet devised a concept, nor even a name, for the union of opposites through the middle path, that most fundamental item of inward experience, which could respectably be set against the Chinese concept of Tao. (Jung, 1953b, p. 203, first emphasis added)

In the *I Ching*, Jung found an approach to understanding the world which was closely aligned with his theory of synchronicity. He observed that Western science is almost exclusively concerned with establishing causal connections between events, whereas the *I Ching* is concerned with meaningful coincidence. This type of coincidence is the essence of Jung's theory of synchronicity.

The Taoist conception of the relationship between the "inner and outer worlds" is easier to understand if we realize that "The achievement of Taoism is not merely that of the concept of unity of dualities or the identification of opposites. For the Taoist there is also a unity in multiplicity, a wholeness in parts" (Chang Chung-yuan, 1970, p. 33). This holographic conceptualization of the world means that Taoism maintains there is a meaningful pattern which underlies the multiplicity, a hidden unity which ties together diverse elements that may have no apparent causal relationship.

Furthermore, for there to be a wholeness in parts means that the configuration of local events in a given moment contains information about the nature of the larger whole. That is why the yarrow stalks may be used for divination when consulting the *I Ching*: the seemingly random alignment of the stalks are in fact ordered by nature and may, to the discerning inquirer, reveal aspects of the world.

For Jung, as for the Taoist, the coming together of inner experience and outer circumstance is a meaningful, though not necessarily causally related, event. Thus, following the Tao and the process of individuation, each require the reconciliation of conflicting parts of the psyche as well as an awareness of and a harmonious blending with the rhythms of nature.

The information revealed by consulting the *I Ching*, or by synchronistic events, is not accessible strictly through intellectual analysis; rather it must be gained through direct, intuitive experience. When the distinction between subject and object vanishes, or when intrapsychic opposites are united, then one understands the Tao.

Taoism: Mindell

Mindell considers Taoism, particularly as presented in the *I Ching* and Lao Tsu's *Tao Te Ching* to be the most complete process theory of which he is aware.

In his workshops and books, Mindell often likens Process-Oriented Psychology to Taoism. Both are concerned with the fundamental process that underlies events; both advise paying attention to any clue (even and especially unlikely ones) which might reveal the presence and direction of the Tao; both advise harmonizing oneself with the Tao, however mysterious or irrational that path might appear; and both suggest that a 'beginner's mind' is necessary to stay open to the ever-changing flow of events.

The Process-Oriented therapist attends to discrete signals or bits of information and then classifies them according to the channels in which they appear. Mindell noted that channel structure is an arbitrary means of classifying the information flow, and that such a classification should not be mistaken for the underlying reality, or Tao: "Using process language we can say that the Tao is the flow of events in and between channels. Tao signifies a process which simultaneously manifests in a number of different channels" (Mindell, 1985a, p. 91). Mindell, like Jung. also likens the background process, or Tao, to archetypes:

> The archetype is the connecting pattern organizing spontaneous events. Thus dreams would be a channel of the archetype since one has minimal control over them. Body problems which cannot be influenced in a causal manner would be another channel of the archetype. Spontaneous acts of fate also belong to the description of the archetype. We see that the archetype is a total picture of the spontaneous phenomena occurring in all possible channels. (1985a, p. 101)

In the *Tao Te Ching*, Lao Tsu wrote, "The Tao that can be told is not the eternal Tao" (1972, Verse 1). This statement, which cautions us not to mistake our ideas about reality for reality itself, is a key directive for the Process-Oriented Therapist. Rather than view the client through the filter of preconceptions, the process worker must maintain a beginner's mind. This is the only way the process worker can hope to track the ever-changing flow of signals, and thus gain an understanding of the flow of the Tao, or the archetypes shaping the over-all process.

This does not mean that the Process-Oriented therapist neglects analysis in favor of direct experience. At one point, it may be appropriate to simply experience the Tao, while at another point the Tao may call for critical analysis. By maintaining awareness and a flexible approach, by balancing action and nonaction, the process worker strives to recognize and support the Tao as it manifests in the client's process.

> ... Understanding and being open to all things,
> Are you able to do nothing?
> Giving birth and nourishing,
> Bearing yet not possessing,
> Working yet not taking credit,
> Leading yet not dominating,
> This is the Primal Virtue.   (Lao Tsu, 1972, Verse 10)

Historical Foundations: Alchemy

The Historical Background of Alchemy

Alchemy has been practiced for several thousand years, and flourished between the 9th and 17th centuries. Practitioners came from all segments of society, ranging from common laborers to kings, and including such notables as Roger Bacon, St. Thomas Aquinas, and Isaac Newton.

The outward or exoteric practice of alchemy consisted of attempts to create the *philosopher's stone*. This stone was believed to have the power of transmuting the base metals - lead, tin, copper, iron and mercury - into the precious metals gold and silver. In addition, alchemists attempted to create a liquid, the *elixir vitae*, which could indefinitely prolong the human life. The innumerable attempts to create the stone and elixir were the tentative beginnings of the science of chemistry.

There was also an esoteric form of alchemy, along with the activities that centered around alembics and melting pots,. Esoteric alchemy gave rise to mystical treatises in which the authors used the language of exoteric alchemy to describe philosophical and religious beliefs. It is this aspect of alchemy that was of interest to Jung.

Jung's Approach to Alchemy

Jung believed there was a psychological and spiritual significance to the alchemical philosophy. In his essay on "Individual Dream Symbolism in Relation to Alchemy," Jung recorded a series of dreams produced by a patient who had no previous knowledge of alchemy. For nearly every dream, Jung was able to produce an alchemical illustration or plate that closely duplicated the symbolism of the dream. He concluded from this that the alchemists, as they conducted their experiments, unknowingly were projecting the contents of their unconscious onto the material world (Jung, 1953a).

The dream images of Jung's patient were similar to the alchemical plates because both portrayed a process of psychological transformation. Jung referred to this process—the integration of conscious and unconscious, of the 'noble' and 'base' aspects of the psyche—as the transcendent function. In psychological terms, the creation of 'gold' is the ongoing integration of the personality. In other words, Jung believed that the symbolism employed by esoteric alchemists paralleled the stages of the individuation process.

Jung incorporated a number of terms employed by the alchemists into the standard terminology of Analytical Psychology. Thus, he referred to the analytical work as an *opus*, the analytic relationship as a *vas* (vessel or container), and the goal of psychotherapy as the *coniunctio*, the union of opposites. The stages of individuation also were described with alchemical terms.

Jung was fascinated with the symbolism of esoteric alchemy for a number of reasons. First, the fact that similar symbols could emerge from his clients substantiated his belief that there is a collective level to the psyche. And second, the descriptive language of the alchemists proved to be a rich source of imagery for describing the kinds of transformation that occur both in psychotherapy and in the individuation process generally.

Mindell's Use of the Alchemical Paradigm

In *River's Way*, Mindell wrote at length about the stages, symbolism, and philosophy of alchemical transformation. He drew extensive parallels between the opus or work of the alchemist and the "art" of practicing Process-Oriented Psychology. Also, in teaching seminars, Mindell often has used the symbolism of alchemy when he speaks about the importance of allowing a client's process to "cook."

Briefly summarized, Mindell wrote that the alchemist works on the *prima materia* (defined as the 'imperfect body' or the 'constant soul'). For the process worker the *prima materia* refers to signals that indicate a secondary process.

Having noticed the *prima materia*, the alchemist then waits for the *ignis nonnaturalis*, the natural spark in processes which makes them evolve. The process worker waits for the signal to perseverate, for this indicates that it has sufficient 'spark' to be worth pursuing.

The alchemist then hermetically seals the *prima materia* into a philosopher's egg. In process work, this means bringing an intense focus of attention—both mind and heart—upon the process at hand. The focus of attention, like an egg, distinguishes the *prima materia* from all that surrounds it, thereby, creating an area within which the *prima materia* may safely incubate and grow.

The alchemist then puts the egg into an oven so that it can cook at a constant temperature. In process work the 'heat' is provided by various techniques of amplification.

Mindell then went on to describe various aspects of the stages of transformation, from conflict between opposites to the eventual discovery of 'gold.'

If Jung's assumption is correct that the alchemist pursued his or her quest unconsciously, then this underscores a basic difference between the opus of the alchemist and that of the Process-Oriented therapist. The task of the process worker is to identify and nurture transformation in a deliberate and conscious manner, and to recognize and integrate any projections the therapist may have as this process unfolds.

This, then, is the alchemical 'art' of the process worker: the ability to gently cook a process, using whatever ingredients and utensils happen to be available, taking care to neither burn nor undercook, not knowing precisely what is being prepared, but trusting that the outcome ultimately will be as good as gold.

CHAPTER 2
EXPLORING THE CONNECTIONS BETWEEN PSYCHOLOGY AND PHYSICS

Introduction

At first glance, the sciences of physics and psychology appear to be at opposite ends of a continuum. Traditionally, physics is the ultimate objective science, probing into the essential nature of the universe, the pillar upon which all other branches of sciences rest. It is the ultimate "hard" science.

Psychology is the study of subjectivity, of the elusive, invisible, ever-changing landscape of perception, emotion, and cognition. In some ways it is the ultimate "soft" science.

The Cartesian and Newtonian paradigms support this dichotomy, but the perspective of modern physics does not. According to neuroscientist Karl Pribram, the convergence of physics and psychology is necessary if we are to understand the nature of the mind and the universe in which we live:

> Thus modern physicists and modern perceptual psychologists have converged onto a set of issues that neither can solve alone. If the psychologist is interested in the nature of the conditions which produce the world of appearances, he must attend to the inquiries of the physicist. If the physicist is to understand the observations which he is attempting to systematize, he must learn something of the nature of the psychological pro-

cess of making observations (1978: 15).

One of the unique aspects of Process-Oriented Psychology is the degree to which Mindell has integrated the discoveries of modern physics with the theoretical and practical aspects of process work. Mindell earned an M.S. in Physics before studying Jungian psychology, and has been working on this integration for over 20 years. In the foreword to his Ph.D. dissertation in psychology Mindell wrote:

> . . . I concentrated my studies in college on physics, only to become dissatisfied with the scientific lack of concern for the personal aspect of events. Hoping to find a more holistic approach, I studied depth psychology. I still remember one of my first dreams in analysis. I was sitting listening to a lecture by Dr. Jung. After the lecture he approached me and said: "Don't you know what you should be doing with your life?!" "No," I replied. "Find the connections between psychology and physics," he declared (1976: i).

In creating Process-Oriented Psychology, Mindell has relied to a great extent upon the theories of modern physics. In the following sections, I briefly outline classical and modern physics, and then describe several themes Mindell has pursued, including: process as a unifying concept, the incorporation of relativity theory, the adoption of a phenomenological attitude, the perspective of modern physics on the body, and the individual's relationship to the world.

Classical Physics

The central figure in the development of classical physics was Sir Isaac Newton. Newton synthesized the works of Copernicus, Kepler, Bacon, Galileo, and Descartes by developing a consistent mathematical theory to describe the behavior of natural phenomena. Newtonian physics was the most important scientific development of seventeenth-century science and remained the cornerstone of scientific thought for hundreds of years.

Newton's theory made specific assumptions about the nature of the universe. According to Newton all physical events occur within the three-dimensional space of classical Euclidean geometry. It is an absolute space that is considered to be eternally at rest and unchangeable. Time is regarded as a completely separate dimension from space. Time is also absolute, flowing uniformly from the past to the present and on into the future. All changes in the physical universe can be measured as a function of time.

Newton believed the fundamental building blocks of the material world to be small, solid and indestructible pieces of matter. All matter was considered to be homogeneous, i.e., made of the same substance. One material differed from another because the basic particles were more or less densely packed.

All movement was conceived to be generated by the mutual attraction of material objects, i.e., by the force of gravity. Newton's genius was that he was able to describe the effects of gravity on material objects in precise mathematical terms. To do this he had to invent differential calculus.

Newton's equations of motion are the basis of classical mechanics. They were considered to be fixed laws according to which material points move, and were thus thought to account for all changes observed in the physical world. In the Newtonian view, God had created, in the beginning, the material particles, the forces between them, and the fundamental laws of motion. In this way, the whole universe was set in motion and it has continued to run ever since, like a machine, governed by immutable laws. The mechanistic view of nature is thus closely related to a rigorous determinism. The giant cosmic machine was seen as being completely causal and determinate. All that happened had a definite cause and gave rise to a definite effect, and the future of any part of the system could---in principle---be predicted with absolute certainty if its state at any time was known in all details. (Capra 1977: 44-45)

According to this theory the individual observer could stand back from the great machine of the universe and objectively describe all physical phenomena. It became the goal of all of the branches of science to achieve such an objective description. Physics became the basis of all sciences, and Newton's model was tremendously successful in describing, among other things, the motions of astronomical bodies, the continuous motions of fluids, and the mechanics of heat.

Modern Physics

Scientific discoveries in the 1800s made it apparent that

Newton's model could not explain all natural phenomena. Nonetheless, his theory remained the cornerstone of the scientific paradigm until several developments in the early 1900s radically altered the basic tenets of classical physics. Of principle importance were Albert Einstein's special theory of relativity, investigations of the behavior of subatomic phenomena, and the development of quantum mechanics. Einstein published the special theory of relativity in 1905. According to the theory,

> ...space is not three-dimensional and time is not a separate entity. Both are intimately connected and form a four-dimensional continuum, 'space-time.' In relativity theory, therefore, we can never talk about space without talking about time and vice versa. Furthermore, there is no universal flow of time, as in the Newtonian model. Different observers will order events differently in time if they move with different velocities relative to the observed events. In such a case, two events which are seen as occurring simultaneously by one observer may occur in different temporal sequences for other observers. All measurements involving space and time thus lose their absolute significance. In relativity theory, the Newtonian concept of an absolute space as the stage of physical phenomena is abandoned, and so is the concept of an absolute time. Both space and time become merely elements of the language a particular observer uses for his description of the phenomena. (Capra 1977: 50-51)

While investigating the behavior of subatomic particles physicists discovered that every experiment they conducted yielded paradoxical results. Eventually physicists realized that the paradoxes were part of the fundamental structure of atomic physics, and that they could not accurately predict or explain results as long as they were following the tenets of classical physics.

One of the basic paradoxes is that the subatomic units do not have a straightforward appearance, i.e., they can appear either as particles or as waves depending upon how the observer looks at them.

Another paradox, referred to as Heisenberg's Uncertainty Principle, is that it is impossible to know both the position and the momentum of a subatomic particle with absolute precision. The more that is known about the position of the particle, the less one can know about its momentum, and vice versa. If either the position or momentum is known with absolute precision, then it is impossible to know anything at all about the other aspect of the particle.

This means that the observer has an unavoidable impact on the phenomena observed. For example, if the observer chooses to know more about the position of a particle, he necessarily affects what can be known about its momentum. The observer is influencing what classical physics considered to be absolute phenomena. According to the Uncertainty Principle, the 'objective' universe is inextricably linked to and influenced by subjective choice. Modern physics holds that it is not possible to be the detached observer postulated by classical physics.

According to the uncertainty principle it is possible to predict the probability that an event will occur, but it is not possible to predict actual events. The paradigm of classical physics held that it was theoretically possible to know both the position and the momentum of an object, and thus to predict actual events.

Quantum theory was developed as a means of explaining the paradoxical nature of subatomic particles. Quantum theory has supplanted the view of classical physics that there are solid objects and that the laws of nature are strictly deterministic.

According to quantum theory, the occurrence of individual events in the subatomic realm is determined by chance. For example, a given subatomic particle (X) may spontaneously decay into other subatomic particles (A, B, and C) whose composition differ from each other. Physicists, using quantum theory, can accurately predict that X will eventually decay into 34.6% A, 49.2% B, and 16.2% C, but they cannot predict whether a given decay will be A, B, or C. According to quantum theory, individual events in the subatomic realm occur randomly.

If quantum theory is concerned with the subatomic realm, what of the macrocosmic realm of everyday, observable reality? Surely there is a distinction to be made between the random yet statistically predictable events of subatomic phenomena and the behavior of ordinary objects such as cars moving on a freeway.

These ordinary events appear to obey the principle of local causes. According to this principle, information is carried from one place to another by a signal, and no signal can travel faster than the speed of light. Therefore, all events must be caused by local phenomena, i.e., phenomena which are traveling at or below the speed of light. This principle corroborates commonsense observations: a light is turned on, and then I blink; I touch a hot object, and then I withdraw my hand. A local event causes another local event.

Occasionally, however, events occur in everyday life which appear to contradict the principle of local causes.

Mindell referred to such a case in *Dreambody*, in which a woman began to feel intense pains in her breast at the same time that her sister, in a distant location and without anyone's knowledge, was visiting her doctor and receiving a diagnosis of breast cancer (1982: 34-5). This incident appears to violate the principle of local causes. Events such as these are easy to ignore because they contradict our commonsense understanding of how the world functions.

Physicists have challenged the commonsense view of the macrocosmic world both in theory and experimentally. In 1964 Physicist J.S. Bell created a mathematical theorem which proves that either the principle of local causes or the statistical predictions of quantum theory are correct, but not both. Because quantum theory has been so successful at explaining everything from subatomic particles to stellar energy, and because a number of experiments have verified the statistical predictions of quantum mechanics, many physicists have concluded that our commonsense view of the world, based on the principle of local causes, is not correct.

But if our commonsense view of the world is not correct, then what is the true nature of the world? Physicist Henry Stapp has written:

> The important thing about Bell's Theorem is that it puts the dilemma posed by quantum phenomena clearly into the realm of macrocosmic phenomena...(it) shows that our ordinary ideas about the world are somehow profoundly deficient even on the macrocosmic level. (quoted in Zukav 1984: 290)

Quantum phenomena provide *prima facie* evidence that

information gets around in ways that do not conform to classical ideas. Thus, the idea that information is transferable superluminally is, *a priori*, not unreasonable. Everything we know about Nature is in accord with the idea that the fundamental process of Nature lies outside space-time... but generates events that can be located in space-time. The theorem of this paper supports this view of nature by showing that superluminal transfer of information is necessary, barring certain alternatives... that seem less reasonable. (quoted in Zukav 1984: 295)

As Stapp alludes, physicists have developed a number of alternative and mutually exclusive theories which attempt to account for the ways that "information gets around." (See Zukav 1984: 296 and Wilbur 1985: 174.) It is beyond the scope of this discussion to describe these theories, not only because they are "less reasonable," but also because the alternative mentioned by Stapp-- that there can be superluminal transfer of information - is the theory favored by Mindell and incorporated into Process-Oriented Psychology.

One of the implications of Bell's Theorem is that the random decay of particles in the subatomic realm is *not* random. Instead, all such events are dependent upon something that is happening elsewhere, although it may not be apparent what the connected event is. That is, the behavior of a subatomic particle is determined by its nonlocal connections to the universe as a whole. Since these connections cannot be known with precision, the classical idea of cause and effect has to be replaced by the broader concept of statistical causality.

The discoveries and theories of modern physics paint a picture of what may be the true nature of the world: an indivisible universe in which "separate" parts and events are connected at a deep and fundamental level.

To summarize, modern physics has supplanted the basic tenets of classical physics. Modern physics is based on the behavior of subatomic particles rather than on everyday sensory perceptions; it regards space and time to be relative rather than absolute; it emphasizes systemic relationships rather than individual, isolated objects; it maintains that we change things when we observe them; it does not assume that there is an objective reality separate from our experience; and it predicts probabilities rather than events.

Process as a Unifying Concept

Mindell conceives of "process" as a common focus for physics and Process-Oriented Psychology, and as a unifying concept for physics and psychology generally.

There are several ways in which modern physics takes a process-oriented approach. Physics, like information theory, evaluates phenomena from a systems perspective, and systems theory emphasizes process over structure. Modern physics thus emphasizes relationships rather than individual, separate objects, and conceives of the relationships as being inherently dynamic. For example, atomic and subatomic "particles" are now conceived to be bundles of energy, and energy is continually active, or in process.

Process-Oriented Psychology also takes a systems perspective. Clients are not viewed as individual, separate objects, but rather as imbedded in a complex web of systemic relationships. The fundamental nature of these relationships is that they are dynamic, ever-changing, and always in process.

As process unfolds, it does so in the form of patterns. In physics, these patterns are described in terms of the probabilistic wave equations of quantum mechanics. In Process-Oriented Psychology, patterns are attributed to the organizing function of archetypes. Both archetypes and wave functions are attempts to describe the creation of patterns out of underlying process. In *River's Way*, Mindell wrote that

> ... dream work indicates that outer events are not haphazard phenomena, but conform to patterns and have meanings. The course of inner and outer processes conforms to the patterns or archetypes found in the dreams of the observer. These patterns create the essence of process, 'process logic.' This logic gives coherence to all spontaneous perceptions. For example, apparently dissociated dream fragments are not independent pieces of some chaos, but cluster around a particular archetype (1985a: 60).

Modern physics no longer considers space or time to be absolute qualities. Physicist David Finkelstein considers process to be more fundamental than either space or time: "classical quantum mechanics is a hybrid of classical concepts (space, time) and quantum concepts (states, tests). A more consistently quantum mechanics is proposed, with space, time, and matter replaced by one primitive concept of process" (quoted in Mindell 1985a: 67).

In Process-Oriented Psychology, Mindell referred to this "primitive concept of process" as the *Unus Mundus*, or one world, a term borrowed from Jung: "The Unus Mundus is the world of archetypes in contrast to the world of archetypal manifestations such as dream processes and synchronicities . . . . (and) reflects a level of existence from which the manifest world is created" (1985a: 63).

Finally, in addition to linking physics and Process-Oriented Psychology, Mindell also considers the concept of process to be a bridge between physics and psychology generally:

> . . . in a post-Einsteinian universe, where telepathy, synchronicity, dreams, and somatic body trips occur, the concept of process unifies events which move from psyche to matter, imaginations into the body. This concept allows psychology and physics to come together and allows the process worker to deal with post-Einsteinian signals and channels, regardless of their inner mechanisms or superluminal nature (1985a: 68).

Bringing Relativity into Psychology

In *River's Way*, Mindell wrote that Einstein's theories inspired him to relativize the channels in Process-Oriented Psychology.

Just as Einstein's theories established that neither space nor time are absolute, in Process-Oriented Psychology, the channel structure is not absolute. According to Einstein, there is a space-time continuum, and in Process-Oriented Psychology, there is a continuum of experience which has been differentiated into the auditory-visual-proprioception-kinesthesia-relationship-world channels (for a description of the Process-Oriented channels, see Appendix

B). None of these channels has an absolute value relative to the others, and no channel exists apart from the others: they are all part of the same continuum of experience.

Many systems of psychotherapy appear to favor one type of channel experience over another. Depending upon its orientation, a school of psychotherapy may favor internal body experiences, verbal expression, movement, or visual imagery. In Process-Oriented Psychology, it is the information value of the experience that is important, not the channel in which it occurs.

In addition to relativizing the channels, Einstein's theory of the spacetime continuum has influenced the attitude of Process-Oriented Psychology toward what is "real" and what is not. As Capra has observed,

> We have no direct sensory experience of the four dimensional space-time, and whenever this relativistic reality manifests itself—that is, in all situations where high velocities are involved—we find it very hard to deal with it at the level of intuition and ordinary language (1988: 89).

In fact, we sometimes do appear to have direct sensory experience of four dimensional spacetime, and occasionally these experiences may occur within the context of psychotherapy. The process worker cannot simply dismiss experiences that are unique or unusual, such as telepathy or a synchronistic event, but must be receptive to them for at least two reasons. First, because they may be meaningful and helpful to the client; and second, because our common-sense notions of space and time are, after all, only relative.

The Phenomenological Attitude

In *River's Way*, Mindell wrote that Process-Oriented Psychology is derived in part from "the phenomenological attitude of theoretical physics" (1985a: viii). (Jung also described his own attitude as phenomenological, so it is likely that this, too, was another influence on Mindell to adopt this orientation.) Traditionally, the phenomenological method is a way of dealing with information that presents itself to human experience. In Process-Oriented Psychology, the therapist takes a phenomenological approach by examining the facts of perception with an attitude of neutrality.

> One of the advantages of process science is its neutral basis. Since process work is based upon a phenomenological viewpoint, terms such as psyche and matter, inner and outer, psychology and physics, are replaced by the experiences, awareness, and observations of a given observer. Thus the physicist's approach to 'purely material' events is, in principle, no different that the process worker's approach to body, dream, or relationship experiences. (Mindell 1985a: 55)

Psychotherapists display the natural tendency to classify perceived facts into specific categories. Once this is done, the inclination is to ignore any new facts that do not fit preconceived beliefs. The Process-Oriented therapist also categorizes experience, but attempts to stay neutral by remaining willing, moment by moment, to incorporate information that runs contrary to expectations. In so doing, the Process-Oriented therapist tries to stay as close as possible to the actual phenomenon without distorting it through interpretation. This is true whether the phenomena fit within a Newtonian framework of clearly delineated cause and effect, or within a relativistic framework of acausal, superluminal signals.

Although Process-Oriented Psychology strives for neutrality, it does not claim to be objective in any absolute sense. Mindell agrees with the perspective of modern physics which maintains that the observer's psychology affects that which is observed. This means that the therapist will always alter what is observed, no matter how close the therapist manages to get to the actual phenomenon.

The phenomenological attitude does not mean that the Process-Oriented therapist remains uninvolved. On the contrary, ideally the process worker is able to participate fully in the ongoing flow of events even while observing what is happening. This is far from easy, for whenever the therapist finds himself or herself at his or her own growing edge, the tendency is to lose awareness. As Mindell has noted, someone who could continually maintain the balance between experiencing and phenomenological awareness would "correspond to a psychological ideal, the integrated or whole individual, someone who is simultaneously involved and clear about his involvement" (1985a: 66).

Modern Physics and the Body

Mindell's understanding of modern physics has influenced the way in which he conceptualizes body phenomena.

Modern physics maintains that an observer affects that which is observed. Just as light resembles either a particle or a wave depending upon the nature of the observational process, so too the body takes on different appearances according to the way in which it is viewed. For example, if blood is drawn and analyzed, then the body is perceived in terms of blood chemistry. To an athlete running a race, the body consists of a medley of proprioceptive and kinesthetic sensations.

Mindell has referred to the body observed through objective physiological measurements as the 'real body,' while the body observed through individual experience is the 'dreambody.'

Typically, the measurements of the real body are considered to be more objective and valid than the body as perceived by individual experience. And yet the real body can no longer be considered to be absolute, for several reasons. The first reason is that the subjectivity of the observer affects all observations, so that every measurement becomes relative. Secondly, if physicists view matter as energetic fields of varying intensities rather than solid, clearly defined particles, then we can no longer assume that the 'real body' is simply a solid object with objectively measurable qualities.

Just as a physicist must be able to view light as both particle and wave, so Mindell considers both the real body and the dreambody to be equally valid:

> Both real body and dreambody descriptions are valid within their own observational realm. Confusion arises only when one body description is treated more importantly than the other or when questions pertaining to one body are asked about the other body (1982: 10-11).

Mindell thus recognizes the 'real' body of objective physiological measurements as well as the dreambody of individual experience, and does not consider one to be more important or 'real' than the other. Valuable information would be overlooked if either the real body or the dreambody is not thoroughly investigated.

Applied to the practice of psychotherapy, this means that if a client reports that the client has high blood pressure, and also remarks that the beating of the client's heart is like the pounding of an anvil, then each of these statements reveals something about the nature of the client's body. Taking the first statement seriously might mean encouraging the client to continue to have the client's blood pressure monitored. Taking the second statement seriously might mean having the client amplify the client's experience of the pounding anvil, and thereby discover more about the nature of the dreambody.

In a later work, Mindell (1989a) further differentiated the categories of body experience.

The Individual's Relationship to the World

The theories of modern physics maintain that individuals do not exist in isolation from all other people and from the world. Mindell has used field theory and the analogy of the hologram to explain how the consciousness and destiny of the individual is inextricably linked to global and universal processes.

Field Theory

Mindell's inclusion of a world channel in the channel structure of Process-Oriented Psychology is critical to his theoretical explanations of synchronicity, dreaming up, and the nature of mental illness. The world channel includes the individual's relationship to unfamiliar people, and to collective groups of people, such as community, country, and foreign nations. It also includes the individual's relationship to inorganic phenomena such as physical objects and the universe.

Mindell has included a world channel because he noticed that different aspects of the world sometimes behave as though they are part of an individual's process. Information can be transferred to the individual via the world channel in a number of ways. In the case of dreaming up, the information is transmitted by another person. In the case of some synchronistic events, the information appears in the form of animals or natural phenomena. In some cases, such as telepathy, the transfer of information from the world to the individual does not obey the principle of local causes.

The behavior of the world as a channel for the individual has led Mindell to speculate about the field-like properties of the human mind. As the examples above indicate, "our mind can be spread over space at any given moment" (Mindell 1989b: 56). In other words, whereas the physical brain is located in the human skull, the mind behaves like a field of consciousness that extends throughout both local and nonlocal space. Each person is an individual whose field includes other individuals and the world at large.

This same field-like quality also is characteristic of the world itself, so that the "world is a field, organized by patterns, not by time and space" (Mindell 1989b: 56). The world's field is inextricably linked with the fields of individuals. Just as the world can be a channel for the individual, so too is the individual a channel for the global field, which Mindell refers to as the global dreambody. Every person is simultaneously an individual dreambody and part of the collective dreambody.

> Thus an individual can be considered as the unconscious or the split-off and dreamed-up part of another person or group just as the group can be understood as a part of the individual. If we switch our viewpoints and no longer consider the individual and his dream as the center of the universe, but the universe's process as the central phenomenon organizing the behavior of its individual parts, we enter that part of psychology which borders upon relativistic physics. (1985a: 54)

The Hologram

In addition to having a field-like aspect, another way of describing the interrelatedness of the individual and the world is by using the analogy of the hologram.

Hologram theory was originally developed in the late 1940s by Nobel physicist Dennis Gabor, but it was not until the invention of the laser that it became possible to create holographic images. A hologram is a special kind of optical storage system in which an image of the whole is encoded in each of the parts. For example, suppose a holographic photograph is taken of a tree, and then the image of a branch is cut away. If the image of the branch is then enlarged to the size of the original photograph the resulting picture will be of the entire tree, not just an enlarged branch. In other words, each individual part of a holographic image is a condensed representation of the entire image.

In physics one of the leading proponents of a holographic model of the nature of reality and consciousness is David Bohm (1980). Bohm's theory is an attempt to account for the difference between the manifest world of appearances, in which objects appear separate and distant, and the underlying, hidden reality, which is indivisible and connected. Bohm refers to the phenomenal world, in which objects and events that appear to be separate and discrete in space and time, as the explicate or unfolded order. The explicate realm is contained within and generated by a more fundamental realm of undivided wholeness which he terms the implicate or enfolded order. Because the implicate whole is available to each explicate part, Bohm's model is a holographic one.

A holographic model of the universe depicts the relationship of a part to the whole in a very different manner than the Newtonian, mechanistic model. The Newtonian model emphasizes substance and quantity, so that there is a clear difference between, for example, a single cell and the entire body of which it is a part. The holographic model emphasizes information, so that a single cell, through its genetic code, contains information about the entire body.

Mindell has applied the holographic model to various aspects of human behavior and experience:

The world we live in behaves, in many respects, like a

hologram. It's broken up into little segments: nations, cities, religions, groups, or families, and each of these smaller segments carries the same pattern found in the world as a whole (1987: 99).

In discussing the treatment of the mentally ill, Mindell noted that according to hologram theory the inner personal situation of the client is a reflection of the outer situation in the environment, and vice versa. This perspective gives the therapist several treatment options:

> Seeing the world through the analogy of hologram theory helps you understand how you can change the individual by working with the world or change the world by working with the individual. Thus there are two ways of working with hopeless situations, extreme states, and impossible clients. One is by improving the psychotherapy of the individual and the other is by working on the world situation (1988: 101).

Synchronicity, dreaming up, and projection can also be viewed as holographic phenomena since each of them involve the mirroring of an inner psychological situation by an external event.

Finally, from a holographic perspective, our individual problems and joys are also an expression of a more global process. Mindell wrote that "Your dreambody is yours, yet it's not yours. It's a collective phenomenon, belonging to nature and the world around you. Your dreambody is you, but it's also the entire universe" (1985b: 71).

Thus both field theory and holographic theory point to the same conclusion: that any separation between the individual and the world is in some essential way an illusion.

CHAPTER 3
THE IMPORTANCE OF INFORMATION THEORY TO PROCESS WORK

Introduction

In his Acknowledgments to *River's Way*, Arnold Mindell wrote that Process Work is derived in part from electronic communication theory (viii). Communication theory is also known as cybernetics, information theory, or systems theory. In this book I use the more common term information theory.

One way of describing Process Work is that it is a signal-based system of psychotherapy. According to Goodbread, a signal is "any discrete piece of information which is perceived by the client, the therapist or both" (1987: 154). The integration of information theory into Process Work is of central importance in understanding how a Process Worker classifies and interprets perceived signals.

I will summarize the basic principles of information theory, and then describe how Mindell has incorporated these concepts into Process Work.

The Development Of Information Theory

According to Bateson (1973) information theory was the outgrowth of a number of investigations of the nature of control and self-regulation in machines and living organisms. These ideas were developed in different countries during World War II. Among the principal investigators were Ludwig von Bertalanffry, Norbert Wiener, John Von Neumann, Claude Shannon, and K.J.W. Craik. When their discoveries were integrated shortly after the war, information theory was born. Although information theory was originally formulated as a mathematical model, it has been applied with great success in fields such as psychology, biology, sociology and economics.

Key Concepts

Information theory is the study of systems and the way that information flows within and between systems. According to Watzlawick et al (1967) the emphasis upon systems amounted to a radical change in scientific epistemology. Until the study of systems, science---led by classical physics---had essentially focused on linear, uni-directional and progressive cause-effect relations. As long as this remained true, then phenomena which were characterized by growth or change could not be properly studied or understood.

Central to the change in perspective was the discovery of feedback. A series of events in which event a effects event b, and b then effects c, and so forth, is an example of a linear, deterministic chain of causality. According to classical physics, the universe was conceived to function in such a linear, causal manner.

This mechanistic approach proved to be very useful, and has been instrumental in significant advances made by science.

The situation is entirely different if the series of events proceeds from a to b to c, and then event c feeds back to a. Compared to a strictly linear set of phenomena, a system with feedback is more complex, operates according to a different set of rules, and requires a new conceptual framework for understanding.

This is particularly true in the case of an **open system**. Organic systems are open because they exchange materials, energies or information with their environments. Examples of open systems include individual organisms such as plants, animals and people; social systems such as beehives or human societies; and ecosystems, in which there is a systemic interaction between living organisms and the surrounding, inanimate environment. A system is **closed** if there is no such exchange with the surrounding environment. An example of a closed system would be a chemical reaction taking place inside a container which was completely sealed and insulated.

Classical physics employed a theoretical model in which the universe was believed to be strictly comprised of closed systems. Within the closed systems were discrete objects whose properties could be isolated and studied. This theoretical model has proven to be inadequate and misleading when applied to organic systems.

From the perspective of information theory, a system is an integrated whole. The properties of systems are derived from the relationships between their parts rather than from the parts themselves. It is not possible to study part of a system in complete isolation from the other parts. Because information theory emphasizes the principles of organization and dynamic flow of relationships within a given system, processes are considered to be more fundamental than structure. Capra has noted that the focus on process and inter-relationship makes information theory "a natural extension of modern physics." (Wilber 1985: 240)

As Bateson has pointed out, information theory does not study events and objects; rather it studies "the *information* 'carried' by events and objects" (1973: 401). The information value of an event or object is determined by its probability. In other words, any event that is routine or expected generally does not contribute very much information, whereas events which are new or unexpected have a relatively high information value.

Information Theory and Process Work

Recognition of the Fundamental Importance of Process

As indicated by its very name, in Process Work, as in information theory, processes are regarded as more fundamental than structure.

Mindell defined process as the variation of signals experienced by an observer. He contrasted process with the idea of a fixed state, which is "an unchanging description of a situation which has been broken up into parts" (1985a: 11).

A state-oriented psychology would tend to create fixed descriptions of subsets of human experience, and would then be inclined to perceive clients in terms of these descriptions. The drawback in this approach is that, for example, a state-oriented therapist might insist upon a specific procedure for healing a client, and would be likely to miss or ignore signals indicating that the procedure was not accurately recognizing or addressing the uniqueness of the client.

The Process Worker forms hypotheses about the

nature of therapeutic interactions, but must be prepared to discard the hypotheses immediately when they do not match what is occurring in the session. It is important to recognize the value of following a fixed routine when it is appropriate to do so, and then being alert enough to notice and respond to any anomalies in a routine pattern. In this way the Process Worker attempts to recognize and respond to the dynamic and changing flow of events.

Emphasis Upon Principles of Organization

Information theory focuses upon the principles of organization of a given system. Process Work does this by attempting to determine the process structure of a therapeutic interaction.

A Process Worker follows the flow of information by noting specific signals and classifying them according to the channels in which they are occurring. The Process Worker notes what the client does and does not identify with and classifies it in terms of primary and secondary process. By emphasizing process structure, and by employing terms such as channel and signals, Mindell is utilizing the language and epistemology of information theory.

The Systems Perspective

For many years, modern psychology did not attempt to take a systems view, in part because it emerged from and relied upon the epistemology of the predominant scientific disciplines. In the 18th and 19th centuries, physics and chemistry used the Cartesian-Newtonian epistemology to great effect. In the early years of this century, psychology sought to be equally rigorous, and the results were reflected in both the assumptions and language of psychotherapy. Influenced by Descartes, psychotherapy generally referred to "mind" and "body" as though they were distinct entities. The emphasis was upon internal psychological processes as distinct from somatic processes or from interactions with the environment.

For example, classical psychoanalysis is essentially a description of intrapsychic phenomena. Psychoanalytic terminology reflects this bias in that the only term that bridges the gap between intrapsychic events and external behavior is projective identification. This approach maintains the mind/body split, represents the individual as isolated from the environment, and portrays mental illness as an individual problem. It was not until Bateson (1973) employed an information or systems theory perspective that schizophrenia was clearly described in terms of interactions (double binds) between individuals.

Influenced by Newton, psychoanalysis made reference to psychic "objects" being acted upon by "forces" or "energy" in a causal, linear fashion. Adopting the notion of "energy" as a determinant of behavior was problematic. Even Jung, who attempted to incorporate a systems perspective into his view of the psyche, was hampered by his use of the term energy as an explanatory principle.

Information theory maintains that a system is an integrated whole. Process Work clearly approaches psychotherapy from a systems perspective. In *Working With the Dreaming Body*, Mindell wrote:

Looking at my client and understanding his dreambody from his point of view is a very meaningful experience for him. Yet it is also important for me to understand and to see what my dreambody is doing in my dreams, body and environment.

However, now as I talk to you about the dreambody's information system, I'm able, for a moment, to step outside the situation long enough to notice something. Namely, that the two of us form a unity, an inseparable system whose parts can be defined, but not divided from one another. The two of us, the therapist and client, or the two partners of any couple, form the basic particles of a system.

These particles cannot really be taken out of the system and analyzed separately from the field in which they live. You cannot take a child out of its family and understand the child completely. You have to see this child within its family structure to understand it as fully as possible. When there are two people, there are three things happening. There's you, your partner and there's also the system or couple which you create and which behaves differently than the mere sum of its parts (1985b: 75).

Mindell has applied a systems perspective to working with body symptoms (1985b); small group, community and global processes (1989b, 1992, 1995); relationships (1987); mental illness (1988); comas (1989a); and general process theory (1985a).

The Significance of Feedback

By paying close attention to signals, the Process Worker is very attentive to feedback received from the client. For example, suppose a client tells the therapist that the client wants to change some aspect of the client's life. The therapist may then make a suggestion to the client about how this change might be achieved. The utility of the suggestion is determined by the feedback from the client.

Feedback can be either positive or negative. According to information theory, negative feedback maintains a homeostatic or steady state condition. Homeostasis is a way of achieving and maintaining stability and predictability in relationships. If the client responds negatively to the therapist's suggestion, then the Process Worker recognizes that he or she must try another alternative if he or she is to support the client's desire to change.

If the client responds positively, then the therapist knows that this is the correct route to follow. According to information theory, positive feedback leads to a loss of equilibrium and results in change.

Feedback from the client indicates the most appropriate way for the client to change. Feedback tells the Process Worker how to adapt his or her approach to the idiosyncratic needs of the client. This is in contrast to a "state-oriented" approach in which the therapist follows a set program without regard for the client's feedback. In addition, by noticing and responding to feedback the Process Worker is modeling an open system for the client.

The Information Value of Events

Information theory is concerned with the information value of events rather than the events themselves.

Mindell's emphasis on information enables him to avoid relying upon terms such as energy when discussing the nature of psychotherapeutic interactions. Focusing on information and identifying a wide range of channels in which signals occur allows the Process Worker to track a process as it manifests in different aspects of the interactive system.

The appearance of an information-laden signal in successive channels is known as "channel switching," and is an example of what Mindell has referred to in teaching seminars as the conservation of information. For example, a Process Worker may observe that a client is having a strong proprioceptive experience. When the proprioception has proceeded as far as it can in that channel, it may then switch to a vision. This may in turn switch to a movement, and so forth. The information content of the original signal is being conserved, even while the channel in which the information is occurring is changing. It is the information being "carried" by the feeling, vision, or movement that is of primary importance. This approach is extremely flexible and allows the Process Worker to track the client's process as it shifts in focus from mind to body, or from individual to society.

As noted above, a key concept in information theory is that the more improbable an idea or event is, the higher its informational value. In process terminology, the signals of the primary process represent that which is ordinary and to be expected. Typically at some point, the client will begin to double signal, that is, will send a signal that contradicts the ongoing message of the primary process. These secondary signals, because they are relatively unusual and unexpected, have a greater information value than the primary signals. The attentive Process Worker will notice the secondary signals and encourage the client to amplify them so that the information they carry will become more accessible. Thus information theory provides a clear rationale for investigating the secondary signals.

Conclusion

There are a number of ways in which information theory is integral to the theory and practice of Process Work. These include:

- a recognition of the fundamental importance of process
- emphasis upon principles of organization
- acknowledgment of the systemic nature of any therapeutic exchange
- focus upon the informational value of events, and
- recognition of the significance of feedback.

As noted in the introduction, Process Work is a signal-based system of psychotherapy, and it is information theory which provides the theoretical framework for understanding how signals flow in systems. Mindell's incorporation of the principles of information theory, along with those of modern physics, brings Process Work into alignment with the modern scientific paradigm, and does so in a manner which is extremely flexible and of great practical utility.

CHAPTER 4

GESTALT PSYCHOLOGY: EXTRAVERTING THE UNCONSCIOUS

Introduction

In *River's Way*, Mindell wrote that Process-Oriented Psychology rests in part upon gestalt-oriented process work, and that "Fritz Perls encouraged me through his games with the hot seat to extravert the unconscious and try to get away with it" (1985a, p. vii). In this chapter, I briefly explain how several of the techniques of Gestalt Therapy succeed in extraverting the unconscious, and outline the significance of this approach for Process-Oriented Psychology.

Techniques of Gestalt Therapy

Perls utilized a number of psychotherapeutic techniques for working with clients. The two techniques that Mindell found useful in 'extraverting the unconscious' are psychodrama and the 'empty chair.'

In psychodrama, the client re-enacts specific, emotionally-charged situations by playing the roles of the various participants in the situation. The roles are re-enacted through verbal exchanges as well as movement. Many variations are possible, including the therapist acting out a role in the psychodrama, role-reversals, and so forth.

In the 'empty chair' technique (which Mindell referred to above as the 'hot seat') the client imagines that a significant figure in his or her life is seated in an empty chair. The client then has the opportunity to speak and act toward the figure in any way that the client needs. After doing so, the client can then take the role of the imagined person and speak for him or her. This kind of dialogue continues as long as necessary.

These techniques are very effective in extraverting the unconscious. First comes the awareness that the client has two parts of his or her personality that are polarized. Each introverted, internalized part is then externalized; it is given a voice, posture, and movements. As both parts are acted out, the polarity between them is heightened. This has the effect of increasing the client's awareness of each part, and of the relationship between the parts. There is a greater likelihood that the parts will learn to live in some degree of harmony, and that the client will learn to integrate their wishes into daily life, as awareness increases and the needs of each part are expressed.

Each of these techniques relies upon the willingness of therapist and client to regard the client's dream or memory as something that is happening in the present. All memories are expressed through the present moment. Instead of simply talking about the memory, the therapist and client work together to enact it, to make it come alive.

Gestalt Therapy and Process-Oriented Psychology

Mindell has incorporated these techniques into Process-Oriented Psychology with great effectiveness. In Process-Oriented Psychology, as in Gestalt Therapy, a great deal of emphasis is placed upon recognizing internalized figures (which Mindell refers to as dream figures) and identifying the polar figures with whom they are in relationship. When both figures are identified, then the polarity that exists between them becomes more explicit to consciousness.

Simply recognizing internal, polarized figures is useful. But it is even more powerful to externalize and amplify them, to give them a chance to express themselves in the different channels of speaking, hearing, feeling, and moving.

If a client feels the need for a process to remain internal, then a process-oriented therapist will support that. But if the client gives positive feedback about externalizing a process, then the process-oriented therapist has the option of using the role-playing techniques described above. In this way, the techniques used by Perls have become an integral part of Process-Oriented Psychology.

CHAPTER 5
NEURO-LINGUISTIC PROGRAMMING: BEHAVIOR AS A WINDOW TO THE UNCONSCIOUS

Introduction

In *River's Way*, Mindell wrote that "Behaviorists such as Grinder and Bandler challenged me to discover the unconscious in their behaviorist's reality" (1985a, p. vii). In this chapter, I describe some of the ways in which Mindell has incorporated the basic principles and approaches of Neuro-Linguistic Programming (NLP) into Process-Oriented Psychology, including use of information channels, emphasis upon sensory-based information, methods of establishing rapport, recognition that people favor certain channels, and emphasis upon awareness as a way of distinguishing between conscious and unconscious.

Channel Structure

The concept of information being conveyed in discrete channels was developed as part of information theory. Bandler and Grinder applied the channel concept to psychotherapy. In *The Structure of Magic*, Vol. II, Bandler and Grinder wrote that

> There are three major input channels by which we, as human beings, receive information about the world around us—vision, audition, and kinesthetics (body

sensations). (The remaining two most commonly accepted sensory input channels—smell and taste—are, apparently, little utilized as ways of gaining information about the world.). (Bandler & Grinder, 1976, pp. 4-5)

Mindell appears to have followed NLP in applying the use of the word "channel" - and the general concept - to psychological phenomena. Along with NLP, Process-Oriented Psychology recognizes the visual and auditory channels and does not emphasize either smell or taste. The NLP focus on the kinesthetic channel has been differentiated by Mindell into the proprioceptive (body sensations) and kinesthetic (movement) channels. Mindell also went on to expand the theory of channel structure by identifying two composite channels, which he refers to as "relationship" and "world."

Writing about the relationship channel, Mindell observed that "Modern neurolinguistic programmers practice Freudian theory in so far as personal relationships between the individual and therapist are avoided because they create dependence" (1985a, p. 40). Bandler and Grinder described their relationship with the client as 'uptime.'

> We know what outcomes we want, and we put ourselves into what we call "uptime," in which we're completely in sensory experience and have no consciousness at all. We aren't aware of our internal feelings, pictures, voices, or anything else internal. We are in sensory experience in relationship to you and noticing how you respond to us. We keep changing our behavior until you respond the way we want you to.
>
> Right now I know what I'm saying because I'm listen-

ing to myself externally. I know how much sense you're making of what I'm saying by your responses to it, both conscious and unconscious. I am seeing those. I'm not commenting on them internally, simply noticing them and adjusting my behavior. I have no idea what I feel like internally. I have tactile kinesthetic awareness. I can feel my hand on my jacket, for instance. It's a particular altered state. It's one trance out of many, and a useful one for leading groups. (Bandler & Grinder, 1979, p. 55)

Bandler and Grinder are attempting to stay within a strictly behaviorist stimulus-response model, one in which only the client is acknowledged to have an internal reality. Such an approach limits the range of information considered by the therapist, and, therefore, the range of available interventions. In this respect, the NLP model is radically different from Process-Oriented Psychology, in which the relationship channel is acknowledged and is considered critical (to varying degrees) to most if not all therapeutic encounters.

A further difference is that Mindell, following the Jungian model, has differentiated each channel into introverted and extraverted aspects. Mindell has described this aspect of the channel system in *River's Way*.

Emphasis Upon Sensory-Based Information

A further connection between NLP and Process-Oriented Psychology is the degree to which each emphasizes the role of the therapist in gathering precise sensory-based information, both verbal and nonverbal, in the different channels.

This is a central focus of Process-Oriented Psychology, as it was in NLP, and many of the specific information-gathering approaches (such as attending to eye movements and the predicates a person uses to describe her situation) appear to be derived from NLP.

Methods of Establishing Rapport

NLP and Process-Oriented Psychology each encourage the therapist to uses the information gathered to establish rapport on both verbal and nonverbal levels with the client. In NLP this is known as "matching":

> To effectively gather information or beginning a process of change, it will always be important to establish rapport between yourself and your client at both the conscious and unconscious level. An invaluable technique for doing just this is to generate verbal and nonverbal behavior which matches that of your client. This is called "matching." The client's subjective experience becomes one of being really understood. (Cameron-Bandler, 1978, p. 64)

This process of joining the inner world of the client is an essential aspect of Process-Oriented Psychology. NLP provided many insights about how to match with precision, and these are an implicit part of Mindell's system.

Awareness of the Channels

A fourth parallel is a recognition of the fact that, although information is being processed in all channels simultaneously, people have different degrees of awareness of the separate channels. Bandler and Grinder wrote:

> How many here now see clearly that they are visually oriented people? How many people see that? How many people here feel that they are really kinesthetically oriented people in their process? Who tell themselves that they are auditory? Actually all of you are doing all of the things we're talking about, all the time. The only question is, which portion of the complex internal process do you bring into awareness? All channels are processing information all the time, but only part of that will be in consciousness. (1979, p. 34)

People tend to be aware of or favor certain channels over the others. In NLP, this favoritism is referred to as the person's lead system and representational system. In Process-Oriented Psychology, Mindell refers to it as the main and unoccupied channels.

The Importance of the Lesser-Used Channels

Both NLP and Process-Oriented Psychology maintain that experiences occurring in lesser-used channels tend to be quite powerful. Bandler and Grinder described this phenomenon as follows:

If you use guided fantasy with your clients, there are some clients you use it with automatically and it works fine. Other people you wouldn't even try it with. What's the criterion you use to decide that, do you know? If they can visualize easily, you use visual guided fantasy, right? We're suggesting that you reverse that. Because for people who do not normally visualize in consciousness, visual guided fantasy will be a mind-blowing, profound change experience. For those who visualize all the time, it will be far less useful. (1979, p. 44)

In the same fashion Mindell wrote:

The main and unoccupied channels are important for the process worker for if he can determine which channel is a primary one and which the unoccupied or secondary, then the main channel can be use to integrate irrational secondary processes. An unoccupied channel will bring the client the most powerful and uncontrolled experience. (1985a, p. 24)

Conscious and Unconscious

Finally, in both systems there is an emphasis on awareness as being the key to distinguishing between conscious and unconscious. Bandler and Grinder advised people not to

. . . get caught by the words 'conscious' and 'unconscious.' They are not real. They are just a way of describing events that is useful in the context called therapeutic change. 'Conscious' is defined as whatever you are aware of at a moment in time. 'Unconscious' is everything else. (1979, p. 37)

Mindell made the same distinction when he wrote that " . . . consciousness refers only to those processes of which you are completely aware . . . .unconsciousness refers to all other types of signal processes" (1985a, p. 13).

Conclusion

At the beginning of this chapter, I quoted Mindell as saying that Bandler and Grinder challenged him to discover the unconscious in their behaviorist's reality. The behaviorist reality of Bandler and Grinder focuses with precision upon a wide range of verbal and nonverbal cues. Attending to this information enables the therapist to construct an accurate model of the client's (often unconscious) inner world. Ideally the therapist then is able to enter that world to facilitate change.

Mindell's greatest debt to NLP is derived from the range and precision with which Bandler and Grinder attended to the client's signals and the use of the channel concept as a means of categorizing the signals. This approach has been critical to the development of Process-Oriented Psychology.

The way by which Mindell developed signal awareness and the channel structure, however, differs considerably from the NLP model. For example, the inclusion of relationship and world channels makes Mindell's model a more encompassing one, so that Process-Oriented Psychology operates from different premises and allows a greater range of interventions. Consequently the way in which a Process-Oriented Therapist interacts with a client could - and likely would - differ in many ways from a Neuro-Linguistic Programmer. Since my purpose here is to describe what Mindell appears to have derived from NLP, it is beyond the scope of this section to emphasize the differences between the two systems in greater detail.

REFERENCES

Adler, G. (Ed.), & Jaffe, A. (1975). <u>C. G. Jung letters, Vol. 2 (1951-1961)</u>. Princeton, NJ: Princeton University Press.

Bandler, R., & Grinder, J. (1975). <u>The structure of magic, Vol. I.</u> Palo Alto, CA: Science and Behavior Books.

Bateson, G. (1973). <u>Steps to an ecology of mind.</u> New York: Ballantine Books.

Bodian, S. (1990). <u>Field of dreams.</u> Yoga Journal, March-April, 66-72.

Bohm, D. (1980). <u>Wholeness and the implicate order</u>. New York: Routledge & Kegan Paul.

Cameron-Bandler, L. (1978). <u>They lived happily ever after.</u> Cupertino, CA: Meta Publications.

Capra, F. (1977). <u>The Tao of physics</u>. New York: Bantam Books.

Capra, F. (1988). <u>The turning point.</u> New York: Bantam Books.

Chang C. (1970). <u>Creativity and Taoism.</u> New York: Harper & Row Publishers.

Goodbread, J. (1987). <u>The dreambody toolkit.</u> London: Routledge & Kegan Paul.

Goodbread, J. (1989). Dreaming up reality: The politics of countertransference in psychotherapy and everyday life. Unpublished manuscript.

Jung, C. G. (1933). Modern man in search of a soul. New York: Harcourt, Brace.

Jung, C. G. (1953a). Psychology and alchemy. London: Routledge & Kegan Paul.

Jung, C. G. (1953b). Two essays on analytical psychology. New York: Pantheon Books.

Jung, C. G. (1959b). The archetypes and the collective unconscious. Princeton, NJ: Princeton University Press.

Jung, C. G. (1966a). The practice of psychotherapy. New York: Pantheon Books.

Jung, C. G. (1967). Alchemical studies. Princeton, NJ: Princeton University Press.

Jung, C. G. (1969). The structure and dynamics of the psyche. Princeton, NJ: Princeton University Press.

Jung, C. G. (1970a). Freud and psychoanalysis (2nd ed.). Princeton, NJ: Princeton University Press.

Jung, C. G. (1970b). Psychiatric studies (2nd ed.). Princeton, NJ: Princeton University Press.

Jung, C. G. (1973). <u>Experimental researches.</u> Princeton, NJ: Princeton University Press.

Jung, C. G. (1976). <u>The symbolic life: Miscellaneous writings.</u> Princeton, NJ: Princeton University Press.

Jung, C. G. (1984). <u>Dream analysis.</u> Princeton, NJ: Princeton University Press.

Lao Tsu. (1972). <u>Tao te ching.</u> (Gia-Fu Feng and J. English, Trans.). New York: Vintage Books.

Lockhart, R. A. (1977). <u>Cancer in myth and dream.</u> Spring, NY: Spring Publications

Meier, C. A. (1966). The dream in ancient Greece and its use in temple cures (incubation). In G. E. von Grunebaum & R. Callois (Eds.), <u>The Dream and Human Societies</u> (pp. 303-319). Kerdeley, CA: University of California Press.

Mindell, A. (1976). <u>Synchronicity: An investigation of the unitary background patterning synchronistic phenomena.</u> Ann Arbor, MI: Xerox University Microfilm.

Mindell, A. (1982). <u>Dreambody: The body's role in revealing the self.</u> Santa Monica, CA: Sigo Press.

Mindell, A. (1985a). <u>River's way: The process science of the dreambody.</u> London: Routledge & Kegan Paul.

Mindell, A. (1985b). <u>Working with the dreaming body.</u>

London: Routledge & Kegan Paul.

Mindell, A. (1987b). The dreambody In relationships. London: Routledge & Kegan Paul.

Mindell, A. (1988a). City shadows. New York: Routledge, Chapman & Hall.

Mindell, A. (1988b). Jungian psychology has a daughter. The Journal of Process Oriented Psychology, 1, 1-16.

Mindell, A. (1989a). Coma: Key to awakening. Boston, MA: Shambhala Publications.

Mindell, A. (1989b). The year one. New York: Viking Penguin.

Pribram, K. H. (1978). What the fuss is all about. Revision, Summer/Fall, 14-18.

Van Der Post, L. (1977). Jung and the story of our time. New York: Vintage Books.

Watzlawick, P., Beaven, J., & Jackson, D. (1967). Pragmatics of human communication. New York: W. W. Norton.

Wilber, K. (Ed.). (1985). The holographic paradigm and other paradoxes. Boston, MA: New Science Library.

Ziegler, A. (1962). A cardiac infarction and a dream as synchronous events. Journal of Analytical Psychology,

7, 141-148.

Zukav, G. (1984). <u>The dancing Wu Li masters</u>. New York: Bantam Books.

APPENDIX A

JUNG AND MINDELL: COMMON TERMINOLOGY

One of the clearest areas of overlap between Jung's Analytical Psychology and the Process-Oriented Psychology of Mindell is in terminology.

Mindell uses many terms which are derived from Jung, including complex, archetype, collective unconscious, amplification, self, shadow, individuation, and synchronicity.

Mindell retains basically the same meanings ascribed by Jung, although there are a few exceptions. The most important exception concerns the use of the term amplification.

Jung referred to amplification as one of several approaches to understanding dreams. The first step was to have the client freely associate to the various contents of the dream. These associations established the personal context of the dream. The next step, symbol amplification, drew upon mythological, historical, and cultural parallels in order to emphasize the universal imagery in the dream. Amplification thus emphasized the archetypal basis of the dream, and made possible another level of understanding.

For Mindell, amplification is a method of working with signals in the various channels. The Process-Oriented therapist begins by identifying the channel in which the client's dream or body experience is attempting to manifest itself. The therapist then works with the client to amplify the strength of the signal in that channel. This has the effect of increasing the availability of the information contained in the signal, in much the same way that a microscope allows a scientist to study the details of microorganisms. The added detail creates the possibility of further intervention and development.

For a comparison of Jung's and Mindell's definitions of the terms listed above, the reader is referred to the glossary in *City Shadows*.

For definitions of process terms that are not derived from Jung, please see Appendix B.

APPENDIX B

TERMINOLOGY OF PROCESS-ORIENTED PSYCHOLOGY

AMPLIFICATION

Amplification refers to the various methods used to increase the strength of a signal in a given channel. Amplification increases awareness of the underlying process by accessing the information contained in the signal. The methods used to amplify a signal vary according to the client, the therapist and the channel.

CHANNEL

A channel is the way in which a signal is represented.

Signals may appear in a number of different channels. Each channel represents a different way of perceiving.

Process-Oriented Psychology recognizes four basic channels and two composite channels. The basic channels are vision, audition, proprioception, and kinesthesia, while the two composite channels are relationship and world.

The visual channel refers to any perception that is based on sight. The auditory channel refers to any information that is noticed as sound. Proprioception consists of internal body sensations such as pain, pleasure, temperature or pressure. Kinesthesia is the sense of movement or lack of movement of any part of the body.

The relationship channel is a composite channel

which refers to experiences in which a familiar person is the central object of awareness. The world channel involves focus upon perceptions of unfamiliar people, and upon collective groups of people such as community, country, and foreign nations. It also includes the individual's relationship to nature and to inorganic phenomena such as physical objects and the universe.

An individual may experience any channel either introvertedly or extravertedly, depending upon the nature of the signals.

See also "**main, occupied, and unoccupied channels.**"

CONGRUENCE

Communication is congruent if all of the signals being sent simultaneously in the different channels convey the same meaning. If the signals convey different meanings, then the communication is incongruent.

CONSCIOUS AND UNCONSCIOUS

Conscious (or consciousness) refers to reflective awareness, that is, to those moments when an individual is not only aware of a process, but is also aware that he is aware. Consciousness implies the ability to metacommunicate, that is, to reflect upon or talk about one's experiences.

Unconsciousness refers to any process of which the individual is not conscious.

The **primary process** cannot be equated with being conscious, nor can the **secondary process** be equated with being unconscious. It is possible to be either conscious or unconscious of both primary and secondary processes.

DOUBLE SIGNAL

Double signaling occurs whenever someone simultaneously sends two signals with contradictory meanings. Generally the individual is aware of one of the messages and unaware of the other. The term double signal specifically refers to the message of which the person is unaware or with which he does not consciously identify. Such messages are related to a secondary process.

DREAM FIGURES

The concept of dream figures is a way of organizing and making sense of collections of signals over time. It is based on the observation that in many cases, signals, particularly secondary ones, appear to be generated by independently operating subsets of the personality. In Process-Oriented Psychology, these independent parts are referred to as dream figures. Dream figures act as though they have personalities of their own, with accompanying voice tones, expressions, postures, and so forth. Dream figures correspond to Jung's autonomous complexes.

EDGE

The edge is the boundary that separates the primary and

secondary processes. The edge represents the limits of an individual's primary process identity, that is, the limit of who the individual imagines himself or herself to be and what the individual imagines that he or she can do.

THE EXPERIENTIAL BODIES

Mindell has differentiated four experiential bodies.

At any given moment an individual is processing experiences in all of the channels. Typically people are identified with the experiences occurring in one or two channels.

The *real body* is the way in which a person's primary process experiences the body. The real body generally experiences body symptoms, such as pain or illness, as unwanted intrusions and a form of suffering. That is why the real body is often referred to as the *victim body*.

An individual who is identifying with the experiences occurring in most or all of the channels is experiencing the *dreambody*. The dreambody refers to the total personality as it exists simultaneously in any given moment in all of the channels. The dreambody is generally first experienced as an intrusion on the real body and is noticed as one or more symptoms.

The *mythbody* is the transpersonal dreambody. Experientially the feelings associated with the mythbody are generally below the threshold of the individual's awareness. Mythbody themes usually have more to do with personal myths than with the ongoing events of daily life.

The *immortal body* is experienced when an individual lives closer to his or her personal myth. The immortal body corresponds to what Jung called the Self. This is the total self, the encompassing sense of being that transcends identification with the concerns of the moment or with a purely personal focus.

FEEDBACK

Feedback refers to the way in which a person responds to a stimulus. In a psychotherapeutic setting, it refers to the client's response to the therapist. Feedback can be either positive or negative. The nature of the feedback from the client guides the therapist in making interventions.

MAIN, OCCUPIED, AND UNOCCUPIED CHANNELS

People tend to focus on certain channel experiences and remain relatively unaware of others. If someone identifies with the experiences that are occurring in a channel, then that channel is considered to be occupied. If someone is not identifying with a channel experience, then that channel is unoccupied. The main channel is the one a person usually occupies.

PROCESS

Process refers to the flow of signals in channels as perceived by an observer. Process emphasizes movement, change, and the dynamic flow of relationships in an interactional system.
All processes are believed to have some kind of struc-

ture. Process is regarded as more fundamental than structure, and is to be contrasted with fixed **states**. See also **primary and secondary process**.

PRIMARY AND SECONDARY PROCESS

Process can be differentiated into primary and secondary process.

Primary process refers to all of the body gestures, ideas, and behaviors with which a person readily identifies, or with which, it could safely be assumed, the person would identify if asked.

Secondary process refers to all of the experiences with which a person does not identify. Secondary processes tend to be experienced as intrusive, as not belonging to oneself, as invasions or interruptions of the primary process.

NOTE: It is important to distinguish Mindell's use of the terms primary and secondary process from the meanings assigned by Freud.

In psychoanalysis, primary process thinking refers to unconscious mental activity in which there is an uninhibited discharge of instinctual impulses without regard to reality or logic. Typical examples include dreams, fantasies, and the magical thinking of young children.

Psychoanalysis defines secondary process as conscious mental activities that are under control of the ego and guided by the reality principle. Secondary process thinking is a rational, logical attempt to effectively meet the external demands of the environment and the internal demands of instincts. Systematic, rational thinking (such as problem-solving) is an example of secondary process thinking.

In general, then, Process-Oriented Psychology assigns nearly the opposite meanings to the terms primary and secondary process as does psychoanalysis.

SIGNAL

A signal is any specific piece of information that is perceived by an individual.

STATE

State refers to a static aspect of a **process**. State-oriented thinking and perceiving is a function of dividing a process into discrete parts and creating a fixed description of the parts.

ABOUT THE AUTHOR

ALAN JAMES STRACHAN, Ph.D., is a psychotherapist, teacher and author (www.alanstrachan.com). Alan graduated *summa cum laude* with an interdisciplinary undergraduate degree, and then earned two Master's degrees and a Ph.D. in psychology. He was the staff counselor at the Stanford Research Institute (SRI International) for 9 years and has been in private practice as a psychotherapist for over 35 years.

After having studied Process-Oriented Psychology with Arnold Mindell for eight years, Alan completed a doctoral dissertation on the relationship between childhood dreams and adult body symptoms from a Process Work perspective.

Throughout his career Alan has taught in university and corporate settings, as well as at professional gatherings such as the Association for Transpersonal Psychology and the Nondual Wisdom and Psychology conferences. For a number of years, he and his wife Janet co-facilitated a weekly support group for people on the spiritual path.

Alan and Janet are co-authors of *The Lure of the Ring: Power, Addiction and Transcendence in Tolkien's The Lord of the Rings* (https://thelureofthering.com). *The Lure of the Ring* explores the nature of addiction and the seduction of power from a psychodynamic and nondual perspective by examining how characters from *The Lord of the Rings* respond to the Ring of Power. It locates them on a continuum of psychospiritual development, and offers an original, nondual understanding of Tolkien's most enigmatic figure, Tom Bombadil.

Given his longstanding interest in exploring the intersection between psychology, spirituality and politics, Alan is writing a book, provisionally entitled ***The Psychology of Liberation and the Liberation of Psychology: Reclaiming the Revolutionary Heart of Psychotherapy.*** In it he explores the core values of psychotherapy, emphasizing that psychotherapy is a form of spiritual practice in which adherence to its core values not only clarifies and deepens the work but also expands it beyond the confines of the consulting room. Psychotherapy is based on an ethical stance that recognizes that whenever a part of the self or a member of society is rejected, denied or split off, then there is a need for re-integration and healing. Thus, the full scope of psychotherapy involves actively offering empathy, support and re-integration not only for the *disenfranchised or under-represented parts of our psyches* but also for the *disenfranchised or under-represented people in our society*.

When not obsessing about the meaning of life, Alan delights in walking in nature, sharing meals with friends, shaking with laughter, and yelling at the television during the NBA finals.

Printed in Great Britain
by Amazon